Freedom to Fly

From Persecution to Prosperity, A Life Story of Salvation

By Melody Crosby Hale

And Rick & Laura Suhm

DORRANCE PUBLISHING CO
EST. 1920
PITTSBURGH, PENNSYLVANIA 15238

Dorrance Publishing Co
585 Alpha Drive
Pittsburgh, PA 15238
Visit our website at *www.dorrancebookstore.com*

ISBN: 979-8-88729-222-9
eISBN: 979-8-88729-722-4

Dedication

This book is dedicated to those who want to become more than just another statistic; to those who want more for themselves and their families than disappointment and turmoil, and to those who are looking for an opportunity to change what drug addiction is doing in their lives. The influence of drugs in our world has grown to epidemic proportions. We pray this book can provide hope and encouragement, and that it may give the courage and strength to rise above and live your best life! You deserve to live your life with respect, fulfillment, and joy!

Introduction

Freedom to Fly is a collaboration. It is essentially a testimonial interview with Melody Crosby Hale, a special woman who came into the lives of our family. This book includes a study guide to assist anyone wanting to make a change in his or her life. And, the back of the book is complete with inspired devotionals created by Melody.

My wife and I live in Louisiana, and we have four grown children between us, being a blended family. We have a happy life, but our past wasn't easy. My wife dealt with extreme hardship and devastation when her first husband battled with opioids and barbiturates, and the battle was eventually lost to suicide. In my past during my lowest point, I struggled with an addiction to alcohol. In addition, my wife and I both have unimaginable stories about drugs and alcohol within our extended families. The common bond between our family and Melody's family is that we have both been impacted by drug addiction in a powerful way.

Something was quite different about Melody, and I had to know what it was. Melody met my wife through a class at our church. Pretty typical meet and greet with a desire to lift each other up by doing a study together around growth for our businesses. We learned Melody owned a house cleaning business and it just so happened we needed some help in that area.

I clearly remember Melody's first visit to our house. She came in with an energy and a spirit that just lifted the entire house. Have you ever met someone who just changes the temperature in a room when they come in (the kind that by merely just being near, you feel better)? It was infectious. This woman came in and just perked up the entire place. Smiling face, friendly eyes, and just down to earth engaging about contributing to your day. It was clear she was living in a place of joy and no one was going to it take from her! Her joy was too genuine to be pulled down.

You can tell when someone has developed devout character. I have been in business long enough to know when someone is putting it on just because they want you for a client, or whatever dozens of other reasons to act so happy. So, we talked and bantered a bit, and I knew "ok, she's the real deal". We exchanged some talk about church and who we knew, and she made the offer in passing "I should tell you my story someday".

I know that people can make bad decisions. I have made many myself, but is there something to the notion that evil actually exists? We learn from the bible that Satan comes to kill, steal, and destroy, but to what extent? What does this mean, and does it exist? I have fought many battles and had many challenges in my life, including having been homeless in my lifetime, and living on the outs with all my family and friends in the past. It all would seem like an unconnected series of events and bad choices, but is there something greater at work here?

I have witnessed some bizarre and difficult situations including people who have died right in front of me, but it wasn't until after listening to Melody's story, that I had come to an absolute biblical understanding of the word "Destroy". It means "Put an end to the existence of (something), by damaging or attacking it".

My question to you is, if your life is worth being pursued to be "destroyed" and there is an evil bent on taking your life completely, why? Could it be that you are worth fighting over? Could it be that you have such potential and capacity that an enemy would rather take you out? Melody could have easily been killed on multiple occasions, died on more than one occasion, or spent a lifetime in the prison system. Instead, something else happened.

What we heard; you are about to read. Thirty-three simple questions with not so simple answers.

An interview with Melody Crosby Hale.

So, we began talking about Melody's upbringing. She went on to describe a family that is probably not unlike many families including our own. She talked about growing up in a caring household with a mother and father, and how she played sports with her sister. In fact, she and her sister were known for their basketball skills. There was no alcohol there was no smoking. I had to stop and think to myself that we are talking about someone who has issues with drug addiction, and I was expecting to hear that this family had all come from either alcoholism or drug addiction in the home. This was not the case; simply put they were an average family with no real bad influences. They went to church on the weekends and there were no (evident) abuse problems in the home. Our interest was growing by the minute because there is no clear path here to describe anything going on in the home that would support becoming dependent on any type of alcohol or drug. But then, like many families that look normal on the outside, sometimes there are other things happening on the inside that nobody else sees.

Question #1

When were your first memories of being attacked, either in your own mind or by outside influences?

Melody had told us in her own words that evil had come early to attack her, and we wanted to know how and why, and how it affected her life at the earliest point to make things worse down the road. My wife and I were not prepared to hear her answer.

I knew something was different with me because I was not like the other girls. Sure, I looked like any other normal girl, but the areas that are hidden from the natural eyes are the areas that haunted me. I had a drip problem, "down there", that no one could see but me. I had to wear pads from the time I could remember. As a little girl I was concerned with issues like: changing on time so I would not leak through my clothes and have an accident, getting picked on for "peeing myself", worrying that I would smell like pee, fearful of changing in front of other little girls, being upset when I knew my pads were expensive, but needed, and having to carry around the baggage of a big bulky pad! Being uncomfortable in my own skin was prevalent, but I had no clue what it meant nor how to process it.

I do not remember how the rape began or how many times it happened, nor how it stopped. But I do remember who it was that manipulated me and deceived me and stole my innocence! I do remember the old, abandoned greyhound bus where it happened. I do remember the heavy breathing in my ear. I do know that if I would have understood what was about to take place, I would not have gotten on that bus!

Protection from outside evil is a must, but even more so, we need protection from the evil that lurks within our own families. When reality sets in, and unworthiness takes root in our identity, it breeds a playground of dysfunction; especially for an eight-year-old little girl.

Attacked in my Spirit?
Being raised in church, I was taught that God loved me and created me. Since I was born with a kidney defect, I bought into the lie, "Since God created me with a kidney defect, He must not love me too much!"
Truth twisted with lies is always a strategic plan from the great deceiver. As a little girl, I was the perfect target, feeling defective, depleted, un-protected and unloved by God and others.

My wife and I went to bed this night with a heavy heart. But still I remember back to when we first met. Melody was not depressed, conducting her day in a bad temperament, or showing any indication of anything bad happening in her past. To the contrary, all we saw was this extraordinarily strong and encouraging lady to everyone around her. To her now, it was just like telling a story of "Once Upon a time". I clearly understood, but this was just the beginning of her story, and there was much more to come. Melody at some point chose to quit condemning herself and others. How does that happen? We had to hear more.

Other than what you just spoke about, what was your home life like? Share about how it looked on the inside verses the outside.

We had all that we needed but not a lot of what we wanted. From the outside our family life looked normal. Ma's job allowed her to be at home most times which enhanced her homemaking skills. Her role as a school bus driver was to deliver kids to their proper destination and daddy provided for the family by dedicating his life to two careers and learning how to grow a small farm. Daddy was a corrections officer and a military man; correction and protection were in high order. Both of my parents believed in God. Neither of my parents partied. We grew up in church. We grew up being told to not tell our business to others. We were a family of six. We lived a very conservative lifestyle. We grew up on the land, were expected to work hard, and not to ask others for anything. If we wanted something in life, we were taught to work for it.

Daddy grew up in an alcoholic home. His dad was a drunk while his mom accepted the abuse. My Daddy was not able to attend Boy Scout camp because his parents could not buy the food for the trip...because his dad drank up all the money. My Daddy began working at a very young age and was determined to make something of himself. He did not want to turn out like his dad; cold, hard, untrusting, and an alcoholic.

My Ma's upbringing was vastly different. She was raised in a very strict religious lifestyle. Instead of working the farm she begged her mom to let her work inside the home. I can remember Ma telling me that she was allowed to be with my Daddy, alone for the first time, the night before their wedding. I am sure in her parent's beliefs they were doing the absolute best for my Ma in protecting her. Talk about a strict and submissive lifestyle!

Of course, we knew that Ma loved us. She was gentle; and greeted us with hugs and love as we left the house, and as we entered back home. We also knew that we had to walk on eggshells and perform exactly as we were told with Daddy. Maybe Ma in her own loving way was trying to bridge the gap. Either way, a new normal was being formed right before my eyes and I did not know any different. Overly strict discipline from my Daddy and overly submissiveness from my Ma were the right words for correction and guidance growing up in our home. In today's terms it would be called abuse and codependency. Why some events stick in our minds while others are fleeting, I have no clue. But I can vividly remember... I had forgotten to bring Daddy the slop for the pigs and the next thing I knew... the bathroom door flung open, Daddy grabbed me by the hair pulling my naked body out of the bathtub, hitting me so hard that I peed myself while leaving bruises and blood spots on my body. I don't remember where Ma was during this time but as a mother myself, I would have stepped in on this one...or would I?

Daddy took interest in our basketball playing. My little sister is 17 months younger than myself, and we started playing Little League basketball from the time we were knee high to a grasshopper. This was an activity where Daddy was engaged with us. He practiced with us in the backyard. It was not hard having success on the court; between a God given gift and practicing often.

Ma and Daddy would come to our games and having them in the stands meant a lot to me. As we got older, successes meant more than just a Little League trophy. In Daddy's eyes success meant scholarship! It was quite confusing and frustrating to hear Daddy cheer us on in the stands when we were playing great and winning, but on the other hand if we started to make mistakes on the court and fall behind on the scoreboard, we would hear him shouting from the stands "just throw the game away!". It wasn't as if we were deliberately throwing the game away, we were just trying hard to win and not to mess up!

It was evident growing up that God was very important to all our families on the hilltop. We grew up a lot with my Ma's family. I grew up in close proximity with cousins, aunts, uncles, and my Ma's mom and dad. We all grew up in church. Seeing people run around, fall out and speak languages that I could not understand was quite confusing as a child. It was very disheartening to hear from my maw-maw that I was going to hell just because I wore pants or cut my hair. What child wants or should hear that? I lost interest in this God quite early in life even though I was going through the motions of attending Sunday school, singing the hymnals, and saying the prayers. I do remember saying that prayer asking Jesus to be my Savior, but how, as a child, could I really understand my need for a Savior especially when I did not believe that Jesus even loved me?

It was clear that Melody had a mix of normal things and not so normal things going on while growing up. While listening to her talk about this, we could sense that some deep anxieties were present during this time. Self-esteem issues were formed early on, and it was about to get worse. As Laura and I were listening to Melody's story, we could picture the events in our own past where we felt some of the things she was feeling. Melody again was not in bad spirits talking about her story. Her bravery and willingness to continue was overwhelming.

Question #3

Can you tell us what else was going on that furthered your depression and anxiety? I wanted some insight on what her life was like outside of the home and what other factors were contributing.

Growing up with a sibling so close in age had its advantages; we always had each other to explore and grow together with. Growing up with a little sister who was smarter, cuter, more talented in basketball and more laid back had its disadvantages. As a teenager who was very uncomfortable in my own skin, I was eager to find something to do, to distract myself with, to try and fill that hole inside of me. That void would speak louder when I would hear statements from the people that were supposed to love me the most, "why can't you be like your sister?". I had no clue how to like myself, much less be somebody else! The words were like a death sentence that echoed hatred to me. The only comfort I found was in the approval of teenage boys until what I had they no longer needed. It was a vicious cycle of shame and guilt that spurned early in life. It would be a cycle that spoke volumes when nothing else had a voice.

It's called liquid courage, and oh, how I needed courage to face the long days. Anytime I could get a hold of alcohol, I would drink it because I knew the effect it would have on me. I knew that it would not matter what was going on in my life, because alcohol would soothe the discomfort and provide the courage to *just be. I used to get picked on in junior high for having coarse, big hair. I was given the nickname, Brillo pad. There was one guy that would tell me "I'm going to take you home to my mom so she can scrub the pots and pans with you". There was no money to buy mousse to tame the hair down. I hated that nickname. I hated my hair. I hated when ladies would tell me that they wished they had my hair. I wished I did not!*

I was in junior high and had gotten my hands on some Straw-berry Hill and the courage was building. I got some eggs, and we stopped by the house where the boy lived that picked on me the most. I began egging his house and the next thing I knew; some-one was shooting at us. Some of the windows were blown out of the car and I could feel the warmth of the blood on my face. Of course, it was scary being shot at, but I had a voice even if it was but for a moment with some liquid courage.

This was the first time we are hearing in Melody's story that her life itself was at risk and it would not be the only time for her. Things were starting to mount up and escalate. In talking with Melody about this section, she describes a pattern was starting to emerge in her life. We discuss it further and talk together about our similar experiences. Self-doubt and low self-esteem can be a powerful influ-ence. You cannot go through life without experiencing it, everyone has had it at one time or another. How can you develop your character without experiencing this? It is part of life, but why is it so dangerous? Evil wants you to buy into it. The first step of the "destroyer" is to attack you in your mind. Self-disrespect or low self-esteem no matter how it gets there, can turn dangerous in large quantities.

First it starts with a belief in your mind, we'll call "The Big Lie". You buy into it and now believe your life is worth less, not meaning you are worthless, just any amount of worth less than you truly are. This turns into the further marginalizing of your thoughts, and the prospect of giving into suggestions of bad actions some-how gets easier and easier to fill the void of inadequacy. "If I'm somehow defec-tive, who cares how I act or what I do?" We have all had some amount of this, but when extreme it gives the lack of care for ourselves and our actions, that magically turns into a permission slip for doing all sorts of things. It pressures us to do things your friends are doing and to push the limits. Sounds like fun at the time, but more times than not escalates. More bad judgements and decisions follow especially under the influence; just to feel the temporary adrenaline spike, the high, or the opposite, to feel nothing at all. Melody knew that things were escalating and knew the bad decisions were bad decisions, but like many or all of us at times, we just went ahead and piled on bad on top of bad thinking we had it all under control. Meanwhile back at the ranch the people closest to us that love us the most get pushed away. Does the "destroyer" stop there? Nope, the next "big lie" comes and it's all too familiar. "I do not need help from anyone." "I can fix this myself and I'm not telling anybody (who can actually help me)." Does this sound familiar?

Laura, Melody, and I are discussing this and realizing that the first addiction isn't alcohol or drugs. It's the addiction that comes with getting out of bad decisions (emotionally addicted to the high of narrowly escaping something bad, only to test the control of the addiction by doing it again, or worse after swearing to not do "that" again).

Melody is so strong while we are talking and again, we are in awe. She is sharing her story that is not an easy one to share and displaying thankfulness and gratitude. Is it possible that you can be positioned to be thankful for the experiences you have had even if they were bad? We continue.

Question #4

Some people call it "Self-Medicating," did you feel this is what you were doing?

Some people find comfort in food, money, status quo, or relationships... I found comfort in alcohol even though I was not old enough to purchase it myself. Having grown up in a strict environment, where alcohol was not allowed in our home, I would find the loopholes; whether it was staying the night with someone that I could go to town with, or just take a walk down the family street. I was definitely the opportunist when it came to finding ways to engage with that liquid courage that spoke louder than the shame, guilt, comparison, and worthlessness.

No matter what we try to fill that hole in our soul with, it's literally never enough because we always need more. I remember the very first time I smoked weed; I was on the family hilltop, empty inside again, with no alcohol in sight but somebody was whispering words of potential comfort ... "This will make you feel good, why not try it? What could it hurt?" I was already hurting enough.

We were called the Crosby Connection, my sister and me. It was a branding the local newspapers declared over us, a name my family took pride in. When my parents came to our high school basketball games, they each would wear photo tags on their shirts; Becky on one side and me on the other side. I always loved seeing my parents represent me with a smile on their faces. One of the most profound statements my basketball coach ever told us that aligned exactly with the work ethic that my parents taught us was, "In order to win in the winter, you better be playing in the summer!" My parents were so proud of our accomplishments, and I was pleased that they were proud of me also. I did receive that basketball scholarship! It made me feel special and valued just like all the other achievements I had accomplished on the court. But even good things don't last forever!

Finally, I was free to live how I wanted to! I was away at college, a full 2-year scholarship paid for, had my own transportation, could come and go as I pleased, was no longer under the "curse" to attend church and I knew the places that would sell me alcohol. I kept a fifth of whiskey in my car at all times. I prided myself on being prepared for whatever occasion. I lived on campus; looked forward to being on the court, but yet anxiety and escape always seemed to be my companions. For the first time ever in my basketball career, I no longer had my side kick little sister to feed me the ball. It was a harsh reality that I was unprepared for. I was no longer one of the stars on the team. I just could not shake the uncomfortableness in my own skin. I really had a lot still going for me, but I could not see past the pain.

I'm not sure where I was driving to, but I needed to go somewhere because that liquid courage was calling my name. Being in a relationship with alcohol doesn't always bring the warm and fuzzies especially when the jail cell bars are closing in on you. Funny how one can sober up pretty quick when the whiskey is taken away, but yet shame and guilt breed an emotional hangover that can only be cured with that liquid courage that calls out your name just as soon as freedom rings.

After reviewing this section and having discussion with Melody, we are talking about those times where our character and maturity are believed to be in a different place than they are; about how sometimes we felt when we were younger, that we were somehow unaffected or bulletproof and could self-manage our boundaries. It was clear that she knew exactly what alcohol was doing to her and would not accept counsel from anyone about it. Why get help when you clearly have so much control over all of it? Many of us reading this can relate to this notion. We talk about this as being one of the big lies. The first step is to get into a situation where you think you're in control but you're not. The second step is not recognizing any-one that could possibly help. The ones that could help often become enemies because they come from a place where you feel threatened, as if they might influence you to get rid of the crutch, chemical need, or excuses to continue to overindulge. In Melody's case getting a couple of DUI's and being booked in and out of jail was not enough to change anything. So, you may be thinking can things get any worse?

Question #5

When did you realize that some patterns were starting to take place?

They say hindsight is 20/20 and oh how true that is. I could not see the patterns being formed in my life until I stopped, asked God to help me and revisited the past. It is quite shocking to me to have gone through life for so many years and not see the patterns! And it is quite disheartening to realize how a hard heart was being formed right before my eyes and I could not see that about myself.

I was taking a chance on dating a man of color. Growing up in a very small town coupled with family traditions of dating people with the same skin color did throw a wrench into my little life. It didn't matter to me what color someone's skin was. All that mattered to me was that this good-looking guy seemed to care for me and showed me attention. Even when my Daddy found out that I was dating a man of color; disowning me, telling me not to even call home to speak to my Ma, did that stop me! I was determined to do what I wanted to do in life, and I thought it was very unfair for anyone to tell me who I should or should not love.

He was so very excited that we were having a baby. He went around telling people that he was going to be a father. I felt that my messed-up life seemed to make sense, seemed to be coming together, and that we were going to be a family. I needed my own family for I felt so discontented, unloved, and unwanted from my family back home. I never understood why Ma would hide things from daddy concerning their children. I never understood why my Ma would not stand up to my Daddy... fight for me!

I remember finding out that he was cheating on me. I remember saying to him "I thought you wanted this baby!". I remember him saying to me "I want this baby, but I do not want to just be with you!" How could he say that after I had given up my family to be with him?!? That's it! I knew exactly what to do!! Since he wants this baby .... I will make sure he doesn't get it!

My drinking had been taken to another level; why wouldn't it since it was alcohol that soothed the wounds and there were more wounds to be soothed. When the jail cell slammed shut with a 2nd DWI, I knew I needed to do something different. The only thing I had experienced that would bring some comfort to the pain was to smoke some weed. That I knew, would make me feel better. I could not take another chance on getting another DWI. It wasn't until I started penning this book, when re-examining the timeline of relational events, did I notice all of my boyfriends either abandoned me, physically abused me or cheated on me. But there is someone new in my life who is establishing new patterns; He would never abandon me, abuse me, or cheat on me... quite the opposite... a true gentleman! He is written within the pages of this book.

As Laura and I are listening to Melody's testimony, we are still in awe of how humble and gracious she is to share her life's experiences with us. Our hearts are heavy. It was clear that she was having some of the most difficult times that anyone could possibly have, and again she is showing us how grateful she is for it. As I'm taking in her answers to these questions, I am wondering how much do we as people have to experience before we reach up to God for help? There's also the opposite of this question, how much do we as people have to experience before we just completely give up and relinquish our life? Keeping in mind the "Destroyer" Satan himself wanted Melody to give up completely, to be dead inside. Melody states that this was just the start of a spiral that got worse. She is in her early 20's at this point with so much that has already happened to her.

Question #6

To this point have you had any experiences with any other drugs than alcohol and weed?

I had a healthy fear about hardcore drugs like cocaine. I know what you are probably thinking, "Shouldn't she have a healthy fear about any kind of drugs and not touch them?" To me drinking, smoking weed, and popping a few pills was the only thing that made me feel somewhat normal. All the other things in my life seemed to fail me utterly, including people, including religion, including myself! Of course, we all can justify our actions and really believe what we are saying is gospel especially if we have never walked in other people's shoes. I had heard of a well-known and respected basketball player who died from a cocaine overdose just days after signing a contract. That was scary to me because if he could die from a drug overdose, little old me certainly could. I would never touch cocaine!

We were out at the local bar dancing, drinking, and having a good time. I always enjoyed partying because it kept my mind from thinking too much. I knew I could not drink as much as I wanted to because I had to drive later, so I entertained the red pill that was being passed around. I woke up outside lying on the ground unconscious, unresponsive, dying with paramedics working on me. Apparently, I had had a seizure. Of course, I was not honest with the paramedics and was just stable enough not to go to the hospital. I told myself I'd never take that kind of pill again! But there were other pills! I was an anxious person who needed something to help me cope. I continued under the belief that this seizure was just a fluke.

This is the third time in listening to Melody's story that her life could have easily been taken in a blink. She could have been dead that night.

Question #7

You mentioned that things had escalated again around the age of 23.
Can you describe those events to us?

Of course, I was attracted to him; he was tall, dark skinned, dark haired, and had a mustache and big brown eyes. I knew I wanted to go home with him and thanked my cousin for setting us up! Alcohol was a big part of his life, so I fit right in. He was completely opposite of me; shy, not talkative, reserved, and laid back. But let him get mad about something and another side of him came roaring out. I was used to that for I grew up with a Daddy who was angry, explosive, and abusive. I shrugged it off ... I could help him!

When it was good it was really good, but when it was bad it was really bad; harsh words were spoken, things were broken, but making up was so much fun!! Not only was I a runner from the things that were hard in life, but I was a fighter when I wanted something bad enough. I kept telling myself we could work this out, a baby was on the way...wouldn't that change him?

As soon as I found out that I was pregnant, I didn't pick up another cigarette, another drink, another pill, or another hit of weed. I took care of myself eating healthy and walking every day after work. After all I was getting married to the love of my life! Bethany was a healthy 7.5 pounds. She was already loved by many, and it was time to celebrate. I called my friend and she brought me some pills and cigarettes to the hospital.

The very first time that he gave me a black eye I was holding our baby. He had gone to the river and was supposed to be back way sooner. When he walked into the house, I told him to pack his bags and leave. I was tired of him not showing me that he loved me. I was tired of feeling all alone. As soon as I realized he hit me, I left. I went to my friend's house. I needed to get loaded! I needed not to feel what I was feeling. Then I heard a knock on the door, and I heard his voice. He was there wanting me back and begging me to come home! My heart melted and I made way for our house as if nothing had happened.

It is easy to say that we wouldn't allow people to treat us any different than the way we expect to be treated. It's easy to say that we would leave an abusive husband. It's easy to say that I would quit drinking if it was causing problems. It's easy to say that I would never cheat on my husband. It's easy to say that I would never "______" until we walk in those shoes surrounded by all the circumstances of that journey.

I learned quickly about that look in his eyes. I learned that when he got mad, rage churning inside and about to rear its ugly head, his eyes would change right in front of me. So, instead of cowering I started standing up for myself. If we were arguing about something and I noticed that change in his eyes I would do whatever I had to do to keep him off of me. I was not going to be the only one carrying around a black eye.

I thought about leaving lots of times. I wanted more than the way it was. He put hunting, the river, fishing, and himself ahead of me and I knew it. I had so much resentment within myself and the only thing I knew that would change that feeling was alcohol, weed, and anxiety pills. But even those things quit working as well as they had been, so I began looking for something more.

My sister and her friend came over to play poker one night. We were having a good time partying, but I was emotionally and physically exhausted. I knew I needed to go to bed. I was told that if I took some pain pills that it would give me energy and I would feel good. Energy and feeling good was exactly what the doctor was ordering! That night I was introduced to my best friend!! A new camaraderie was forming, and I felt like super-woman ready to take on the whole world, meanwhile I was dying inside.

Question #8

How did this new best friend affect you down the road?

I got off from work, headed home and began physically hurting. My back was killing me. I couldn't understand why my back was hurting because I had not hurt it. And then I remembered what could help! I made the call, picked up the pain pills and the pain went away. Not only did the pain go away but it relieved the resentment I had at the moment towards my husband and to-wards myself. It did not matter if Robert came home on time, it did not matter to me if I was home when he got home. All that mattered was getting my pills. If I had pain pills then life was good, until I couldn't find any.

I had never seen cocaine. I was scared of it. But I was scared even more of living with myself without some kind of substance to help me cope with the reality of my life. A life that I could not understand how I got here and why could I not get out. I told myself that I would be alright, I would do just a little because I needed relief! A little was all it took and then the fear of cocaine left me. Substances seemed to be the cure-all for whatever I was facing, whatever I needed.

The first time I went to a detox center it was to get my family off my back. They could see something was different with me; I was no longer working, I was no longer in school, and my mother was taking more care of my daughter than I was. By this time, I imagine it could be dangerous to even have my child with me because there were no limits to what I would do or where I would go in order to acquire the high of not feeling, not being, and just existing until the next fix. I began writing hot checks; I kept telling myself I would get them covered and I'm sure of it! The shame and guilt were growing at an excruciating pace. How could I have gone from being a person that people could trust to someone that people hated to see coming? How could I have gone from being trusted to open a bank and operate a cash till, to writing hot checks and getting arrested!

Melody is describing to us that (up until this point), she had been in jail seven or eight times. We continue straight into question 9 knowing the situation has escalated and that some serious changes were coming in her life whether she wanted it to or not.

$$Question \#9$$

Some time has passed and your experiences with being arrested have happened multiple times. Was there a time where you felt a turning point was starting to happen?

I was told that I could get out of jail if I went and got help for my drug problem. Of course, I wanted out of jail, but I didn't necessarily want to quit using as that was the only source of comfort for all the pain that was within me. I was willing to give it a shot, it was better than the alternative. By this time, I had been in and out of jail several times due to hot checks and theft by fraud.

Drug addiction will cause someone to do things they never would do otherwise! I never would've thought that I would be in the place that I was in; untrustworthy and needing to be locked up because I was not safe to others or myself. Addiction is all about manipulation, dishonesty, deceitfulness, corruption, and hypocrisy. I never grew up saying that I was going to turn into an untrustworthy criminal drug addict! It is something that just overtakes us, right before our very eyes and we are typically the last ones to see it!

I always wanted to be able to control my usage. I thought to myself maybe this time would be different. I was clean and sober while in jail and maybe, just maybe, by going to this program, it would help me. I was off to a new way of life until of course, I had earned a pass because I was good enough! As soon as I was told that I could go home on a weekend pass the thoughts came barging in. "I can go party just a little before I have to return back." It was a persistent thought that I could not escape! But the thoughts that seemed to confirm how much I needed to go get loaded were right there in my mind... "If I go home, I will just be reminded of how messed up my life really is. I will be reminded of what a loser mom I have been to my daughter, of what a loser daughter I have been to my parents, and what loser sibling I have been to my brothers and sisters, of how my marriage was a joke even though I still loved and hated Robert all at the same time, and how my future is so bleak." Why would I want to face that reality? Getting loaded seemed to be the winning ticket, the easier softer way. Until of course, I was caught; had to pay the consequences, and shame and guilt was shoveled upon the mile of manure my life had become!

This program that I was in was a great program to be in; it was a Christian boot-camp program. It was all about correction in Christ! I was willing to give this Christ a chance but the correction part I never liked. We would read the Bible every day. I remember vividly reading in the Bible where it spoke about loving your neighbor as yourself. And I remember thinking how can I love my neighbor, (Robert who is my husband), when I hate him? To me it was a valid question that I did not have an answer for. I did not understand the Bible. To me it did not make any sense! Did I believe in Jesus? Of course! Did he make sense to me? Absolutely not! But then again life did not make sense to me. I just continued to see myself as one messed up young lady no matter how "good" I was in the short times of abstaining from substances. For I would always mess things up!

Question #10

Was there a point of recovery after this?

I knew I needed more help because I was scared to leave the 28-day treatment program. I knew what was waiting for me as soon as I stepped out of those doors on my own. I was reading the Alcoholics Anonymous big book when I came across a statement about "keeping it simple", and the thought came to me to ask to go to a halfway house. I was in! As soon as a bed opened up, I would be on my way to Pineville, Louisiana. Of course, my daughter, Bethany, would need to stay behind at my Ma's. I was comfortable with that because this time when I left her it was to get more help and not to go get loaded.

I needed to get over my husband Robert! One minute I still loved him and the next I hated him. How could I get over him? The only way that I knew of was to divorce him and move on. I applied for a pauper's divorce. I needed to find him so that he could sign the papers. I was told that he was at a camp on the river, and I headed that way with papers in hand. He was there! As soon as I saw him my heart melted. Oh, how I wished we could have had a good marriage like my parents. Oh, how I longed to be loved by him. I was hoping deep down within myself that he would not agree to the divorce, that he would refuse to sign the papers, and that he would fight for us. He took ahold of the pen, signed his name, then turned and walked away. Not one word came from his mouth. I was heartbroken all over again. But there was something different in my response. This time I did not want to go get loaded! I was hurting but I knew another journey was awaiting me.

My parents took me to the halfway house. I was scared! I knew no one in this strange city! I was so homesick seeing Ma, Daddy and Bethany leave. I knew it was for the best though. I was ready to make a change in my life, I was ready to start over, I was ready to do whatever I had to do for my recovery!

The counselor handed me a book and asked me to read it. I looked at the title, 'Codependent No More'. I thought to myself I am not codependent! Sure, I enjoyed being in relationships, who doesn't? I laid it on her desk and told her that it did not apply to me. She handed it back to me and said it was my assignment; I had to read it and do the work that was within its pages. The more I read the book, the more I identified with the stories. Oh, my Lord, I am codependent! I either try to control others or allow myself to be controlled by others. I realized I have more problems than I originally thought. Not only am I dependent upon substances but I am dependent upon people. Sometimes truth is harder and colder than fiction! But I was willing to face the truths about my life for I did not want to go back to the way I had been living.

I was definitely…country come to city. We had to ride the city transit while hunting for a job. I was scared and had never ridden a city bus before. I remember getting on the bus and seeing a place I wanted to apply. It was coming up fast, so I just hollered out to the bus driver that I wanted off at this restaurant. The person sitting beside me told me to pull the string that was above my head, and it would alert the driver that I wanted off at the next stop. Growing up in the country we hollered everywhere we went! This city life seemed to be too much, but it was exactly what I needed. It was far from boring.

We had to work steps 1- 5 while at the halfway house. I loved going to AA and NA meetings, I loved the server job that I had, I loved saving money for my future apartment, I loved paying off my fines and fees; getting my driver's license back, I loved saving for a car. For the first time that I could remember, I felt as if I had a purpose in life and was being fulfilled. I did not love looking at the 4th step though. Every time I attempted to sit down and begin to work on the 4th step, it was too painful. I did not want to relive those wounds. The director of the halfway house told me that if I did not work the 4th step that I could pack my bags and leave. That was the last thing I wanted to do was to leave the halfway house. I began putting pencil to paper and working on those things that were within me.

I remember writing my Daddy's name at the top of the resentment list. I was so mad at my Daddy for making me have an abortion. If it were not for his prejudices, I would have kept the baby. Maybe my life would have been different? As I kept writing, the truth slapped me in the face, "Melody, it was not your Daddy that caused you to have an abortion, it was your COLD-HARD HEART that caused you to have an abortion." The realization of this situation came flooding my mind and I remembered the conversation that my ex-boyfriend and I had. I remembered asking him why he was cheating on me since he was so happy that we were having a baby, and him saying that he wanted the baby but did not want me. It was my COLD HEART that decided that day that he would not even get the baby! The resentment that I had carried towards my daddy for all these years was a lie!!

In our group session, we were talking about dysfunctional families. I told the director of the program that we did not have a dysfunctional family growing up. That I was raised with parents that did not drink, did not do drugs, went to church, and did not run around on each other and came home after work to their families. I remember him saying to me that "Usually in every family there is some kind of dysfunction, and that there is no such thing as a normal family!" I was seriously taken aback by that statement. I began to question within myself what was dysfunctional about my family life growing up?

For the first time ever, I shared about the incident with my cousin! Sure, I was a little girl (around 8 years old), I did not understand what was happening to me. And once I began learning about the birds and the bees in hearing statements about saving ourselves for our marriage, it was too late!! He had taken it away from me and there was nothing that I could do about it! Funny thing about shame and guilt...It's all about a word game. As a teenager, I grew up carrying around guilt and shame because I did not try to "fight him off". I grew up with shame and guilt because it was family, my own cousin! Shame and guilt told me that I was a participant. Shame and guilt told me that it was my fault. Growing up with shame and guilt prevented me from calling the incident what it truly was...rape! But yet for the first time ever, I now have a choice in this whole thing. I can choose to forgive him!! I can choose to forgive myself for believing a lie that I allowed him to do this to me! As hard as the truth can be, it is the truth that sets us free!

$$\mathcal{Q}uestion\ \#11$$

What happened after those programs ended? Describe your life during this time.

I had never lived as a single mother; clean, sober, and raising a child on my own, much less in a town with no family. It was a terrifying, but yet rewarding experience. My young daughter and I were enjoying life and I was enjoying being clean and sober and accomplishing much! I took pride as an independent woman raising a child on my own until life started happening and financial burdens began to pile up on me. The only natural thing for me to do was to search for a man who could ease the burdens. But this time, I was on the prowl for a different kind of man. No longer was I looking for a man's man that wore wife-beater shirts! I wanted something different ....and there he was my guest at the restaurant, wearing a suit and reading a book! When I found out that he was a financial adviser that sealed the deal for me. I was all in. Funny thing though, all that glitters is not gold and money cannot buy happiness especially when sex addiction is in play.

I was clean and sober with a few years of sobriety, serving much in the recovery community. How in the world could I be honest about how my fiancé was wanting to have threesomes and attend swing parties? I can remember thinking, "This is something you do when you are getting loaded, not something you do when you are clean and sober!" But yet, I kept my mouth shut out of fear that my security would go away, and I was not honest about what was going on in my life.

My Ma told me that I was looking to AA as a god. I spent all my extra time at the recovery clubhouses and serving in the community when I was not working. I did not look to God but other humans to guide my life. Sure, I believed in God, but I was mad at Jesus, mad at the church, mad at organized religion! But yet I was making idols out of the AA program, other people... and I could not see that. Denial is not about keeping others from seeing the truth about me, but denial keeps me from seeing the truth about myself. I was blind even though I was clean and sober, but that would not last too long, for the idols that I had created in my life did not have the power to sustain me.

"This hotel gets mighty lonely, and I need you to talk to me," was a fear-provoking statement made by my fiancé that triggered emotional and mental warfare within myself. I was faced with a dilemma; stay home and talk to my traveling fiancé who is living in hotels and needs my companionship, so he does not cheat on me, or go to AA meetings. It was not too hard a decision to make especially when I was not being forthcoming about the mess my life was turning into while I was clean and sober!

The thoughts of a drink eventually came because resentment against my now husband and myself were taking bitter roots! "Maybe a drink will not hurt! I've been clean and sober for so long that surely I can handle it now!"

Question #12

How was your life after this 2nd divorce?

How could I have gone from a life of recovery to relapsing right at four years of sobriety? How could I have gone from becoming trustworthy to untrustworthy again, in such a short amount of time after all it took to rebuild trust? How could I have gone from being a responsible mommy to being a mommy that needed to send her child back to live with my Ma again, because I was incapable of taking care of myself much less another person? How could I have gone from rebuilding my life to completely destroying it again? How could I have gone from being an independent woman to a woman that needed friends with benefits to help support my addiction? I was divorced, broke, addicted, fearful, homeless, childless, and hopeless! Shame and guilt sure know how to take the knife of destruction and dig a little deeper into every wound, into every thought of the should haves. **When we do not understand how much we are loved by God, any self-improved version of ourselves can erode away with each "bad" decision because our identity has become all about our "good" works. When the good works have been taken away, we are left vulnerable and exposed for all the world to see including ourselves where mercy and grace are buried treasures.**

<h1 style="text-align:center">Question #13</h1>

Did you feel God pulling on your heart?

I needed to be back closer to my family because any life that I had built was gone. I longed to be near my daughter! I needed my family, but I was back enslaved to this thing called addiction. All my decisions were based around the need for more comfort that only the drugs and alcohol could provide, never mind the consequences. In my mind, I was already paying the high cost of regret and there were only two things, by now, that I had discovered that would change that: good works and substances. Good works was off the table because I did not know how to dig myself out of this grave of self-improvement when addiction was the driving force behind every decision I was making. Not only was I battling the obsessive thoughts of shame and guilt, but I was also battling the obsessive thoughts of another drink, another drug coupled by a physical dependence that would only let up with more of the same.

I moved closer to home even though I was far away in thoughts, in heart, in actions and in relationships. I needed to find those people, places and things that could provide the means that I was living, not by choice but by dependence. I was nearly out of money. I needed to make a trip to north LA where I knew I could get some more money. I pondered the trip. Why was there a hesitancy to go? "Be still and know that I am God," was a soft message I heard in my mind while pondering. I had enough church services and reading of the Word in me to know that verse came from the Bible. "Be still and know that I am God!" For the first time ever in my life, I had experienced receiving a Bible verse from out of the blue without reading it straight from the Bible. Was God trying to get my attention? I decided NOT to go to North Louisiana even though I knew I could feed my addiction with the resources I had in North Louisiana. But in some weird way, I sensed God was speaking to me. Little did I know that I would get arrested this night.

I had enough AA in me to know that addiction usually lands us in three places: jails, institutions, or death. I was literally dying every single day whether it be spiritually, emotionally, mentally, or physically. Death was there knocking on my door, but I did not know how to escape it. Why was I going to get more drugs when I had some pills? I didn't completely understand that either but what I did know was that I needed more! Would anything ever be enough? Blue lights showed up in my rear-view mirror and off to jail I went.

There was a desire rising up within me to draw close to God and the only way that I knew to do that was to attend church. I knew I needed more than just an AA program, more than just a self-improved version of myself, more than just good works. I was back at my apartment and the recurring thoughts continued to visit my mind about finding a church. I had never attended church in Mandeville. Somewhere along the way, I heard on several occasions about a local church. I did not want to go by myself, so I called my cousin Tressy to come to church with me. We went and I really enjoyed it. While I was in that church service it was as if all my problems had gone away, until of course, I started making way to the door. I remember making a decision that I would be back. Little did I know it would take a while.

Question #14

How did the legal system treat you going through this process?

I was late getting to court because I had been getting loaded all night. When the Judge asked me when the last time I used was, I was honest with him because I knew that honesty was the first step in any recovery program. As soon as I stated the truth, he slammed the hammer down on me with contempt of court. I was completely taken aback. See where honesty got me! I was so blinded by reality that I could not see it was addiction, not honesty, that created this mess.

I was released from jail to go into a detox. I was happy to be there. Maybe this would be the help that I needed. It was not a medical detox, but I was willing to go anywhere other than being in jail. I eventually completed the program and made my way back home to my parents.

I wanted to stay clean and sober, but I needed to make some big money in a fast way. I did not want to have to depend on my family again. The thought came, "I can go back to those relationships that I knew would invest in me financially and be able to stay clean and sober". Little did I realize I was selling my soul once again. It worked for a little while until one day while traveling to Baton Rouge to meet a client, the mental obsession for drugs was waging war heavy in my mind. Funny thing about a war; when one party surrenders, that battle ends, but not nec-essarily that the war is over! When I made a decision to go get loaded, the waging battle ended in my mind, until I was about out of drugs and the war continued.

I missed my court date because I was scared to go in front of the same judge that threw me in jail for contempt of court now that I was back in full blown addiction. I had a warrant out for my arrest and the police were looking for me at my parent's new home in Covington. Now that I was wanted by the law, I could not go back home without going to jail. I could not be with my daughter without going to jail. I took off to live in Baton Rouge. Running was what I did. I was living from hotel to hotel. I ran from one hell right into another.

Question #15

What did you experience while on the run from the court system?

Logically, we would think if something was causing problems in our life that we would do whatever we had to do to rid ourselves of the said problem. Logic does not exist where addiction resides. I did not say nor believe that I would grow up to be an addict or that I would grow up to be defeated time and time again in this thing called life. Did I believe what I was doing was wrong and selfish? Of course, I did! Did I have the power within me to throw off addiction and free myself from the chains that continued to wrap around me no matter how hard or how good I tried to be? Of course not! If I did, I would have never become addicted in the first place! I was driving down the highway while approach-ing an oncoming 18-wheeler. It was headed my way and I was in a little bitty car. The thought came, "Melody, all you have to do to end this mess, where everyone will be better off, is pull over in front of this 18-wheeler. That is all you have to do!" I pondered the option, "It would be better than living in this hell. My family would be better off without me since I am causing so much pain." Then out of nowhere a soft message appeared, "What about Bethany?" My heart softened and the 18-wheeler passed. Was God fighting for me, whispering to me?

None of my options seemed too promising. No matter which way I turned, there seemed to be a dead end, seemed to be more pain, seemed to be more hopelessness. I was so enslaved in addiction that I was doing whatever I could find to put in a needle. My Daddy once said to me, "Melody, we raised you better than this. I do not understand why you are living like this." My most hopeless reply to him was that I did not understand it either!! Who wants to live in bathrooms and hotels intimately chained to drugs, money, and men? As soon as I hit the needle, I knew I was in trouble, I could feel it in my body. Was death here? I came to lying on the bathroom floor with the needle beside me, all alone. Did God just save me, for me to crave the needle again? How can I escape this hell? How could I still be obsessing about the needle when I just OD'd? I really did not want to die; I just didn't know how to live!

Addiction changes people. We do things we would never do if we were not addicted. We say things we would never say if we were not addicted. We become people we never imagined we would become because we are addicted. Does that exempt us from the consequences or the responsibilities of our words or actions? Of course not! Sometimes it is through consequences and accountability that God can bring about surrender. For we cannot muster up enough strength on our own to beat addiction because addiction is stronger than any of us, addiction is wiser than any of us.

There were so many times that God was there with me, protecting me, guiding me, speaking to me but I did not believe it. How could He be after all that I have put people through, after all that I had done, after all that I had said even rejecting and cursing Him, after all that I had become?

Question #16

How did your family and friends treat you differently now than they did before?

In addiction no one wins. Family bonds are broken; walls are erected, and rejection is real. Enablers enable and think they are helping. Family members tend to believe that they can love the addict enough and things will change. People play God and label addicts as weak, who should be able to pull themselves up by the bootstraps. Systems that are supposed to help us, either fall short to accountability or want to throw away the key and punish us into right behaving. Our "friends" are really not our friends. While shame and guilt fuel the cycle of dysfunction. BUT GOD....

<h1 style="text-align:center">Question #17</h1>

Can you describe the first time you openly prayed to God?

I was headed to the dope man's house when emotions were getting the best of me. I missed my daughter! I missed my family! I hated that I needed drugs! I hated the life that I was living! I hated being on the run! I hated how I felt about myself! I hated the person I had become! There were many times in the past that I prayed to God but this time, I cried out to God, "Please... Jesus help me! Please...help me!"

I was waiting for her to come out of the dope man's house when the cops rolled up on me. I knew I was wanted by the law. I knew I was going away. I was headed to jail! As soon as I could get my hands on a phone, I called my Ma. I told her, "Ma, you can sleep now, I am in jail." I will never forget the words that she told me, "Melody, I have been sleeping because I gave you to the Lord!" That statement brought some comfort to me because I knew my Ma had found some peace within herself despite my life. I hung up the phone, crawled on my mat and passed out. Coming to, while in jail, after having been up for days on end, is like living in a bad dream.

There wasn't much I could decipher in my thoughts but there was a memory that kept coming to me: I was remembering how I was on the way to the dope man's house, a few days earlier, when I cried out to God for Him to help me. I was remembering that I was in the block of the dope man's house when I prayed that prayer. I was remembering that I was arrested in the same block of the dope man's house where I prayed that prayer. Oh my, God is answering my prayers!

Question #18

Was God still working on your heart while you were in jail?

Even while being in jail, away from drugs and alcohol, I could not quit thinking of the needle. Being addicted to the needle is just as tormenting as being addicted to the drugs. It's in the preparation; from the drug to the needle, that brought a sense of control to that thing we could not control. The needle was the gateway from the drug to the high. I could not sleep for thinking about the needle. I was not obsessing over pain pills, alcohol, co-caine, money, or men but over a needle. It was the same kind of obsession when one is an escort. The dream of acquiring all that we could ever want, or need is in the meeting of the new client. Until reality hits us dead in the face where truth is so obscured that the life we hoped for was but a fantasy.

I knew I needed to do something to escape this obsession of the needle, but what? It was late at night and all is quiet; where quietness is deafening to the ears, and the obsession speaks loud-est. There were three ladies in the corner, and they were pray-ing. I was drawn to them not because I felt a part of, but because what they had seemed appealing. I crawled out from the top bunk of my bed, went over to the ladies, and asked them if they would pray for me. I confessed to them that I could not get the needle out of my head. I had no clue what they were in jail for, it did not matter. All that mattered at that time was that I needed help; I asked for help, they prayed, and I slept like a baby. Until of course, the next morning...

There was a sense of relief being in jail this time around. The pressures of being a "good" mommy, "good" daughter, "good" sister, "good" citizen, "good" worker, "good" responsible adult was lifted off of me. The guilt and shame of being able to take care of all that is expected in this "good" world was gone. There was nothing that I could go "do" while being in jail for any of those roles. I had blown it and I accepted that reality. The gnawing revelation that was eating at my every being was understanding that no matter how "good" I had been in those four years of recovery, it could not sustain me. I needed more but I had no clue what that looked like!

Question #19

What did the legal system pass to you this time?

The bed to the right of my bunk was neatly made and lying on top were two books: the Big Book of AA and a Life Recovery Bible. I knew the Big Book of AA had helped me in the past to 4 years of sobriety, but I also knew I had messed that up. I was so drawn to that Life Recovery Bible! The title itself, Life Recovery, was attractive to me because I needed a life of recovery, I needed to live! I asked my fellow inmate if I could borrow them. I began searching....

I noticed a group of ladies standing in the middle of the dorm, in a circle holding hands and praying together. These ladies were meeting several times throughout the day. I was drawn to be a part of that. I knew I would need to get up, walk over, introduce myself, and make myself a part of. I was willing! I was asked if I wanted to pray! What, out loud? No thank you! I was there, with them, with God and that was all that mattered at that moment. They closed in prayer, I left the circle and headed to my bed with a peace in my heart. I knew I would be back.

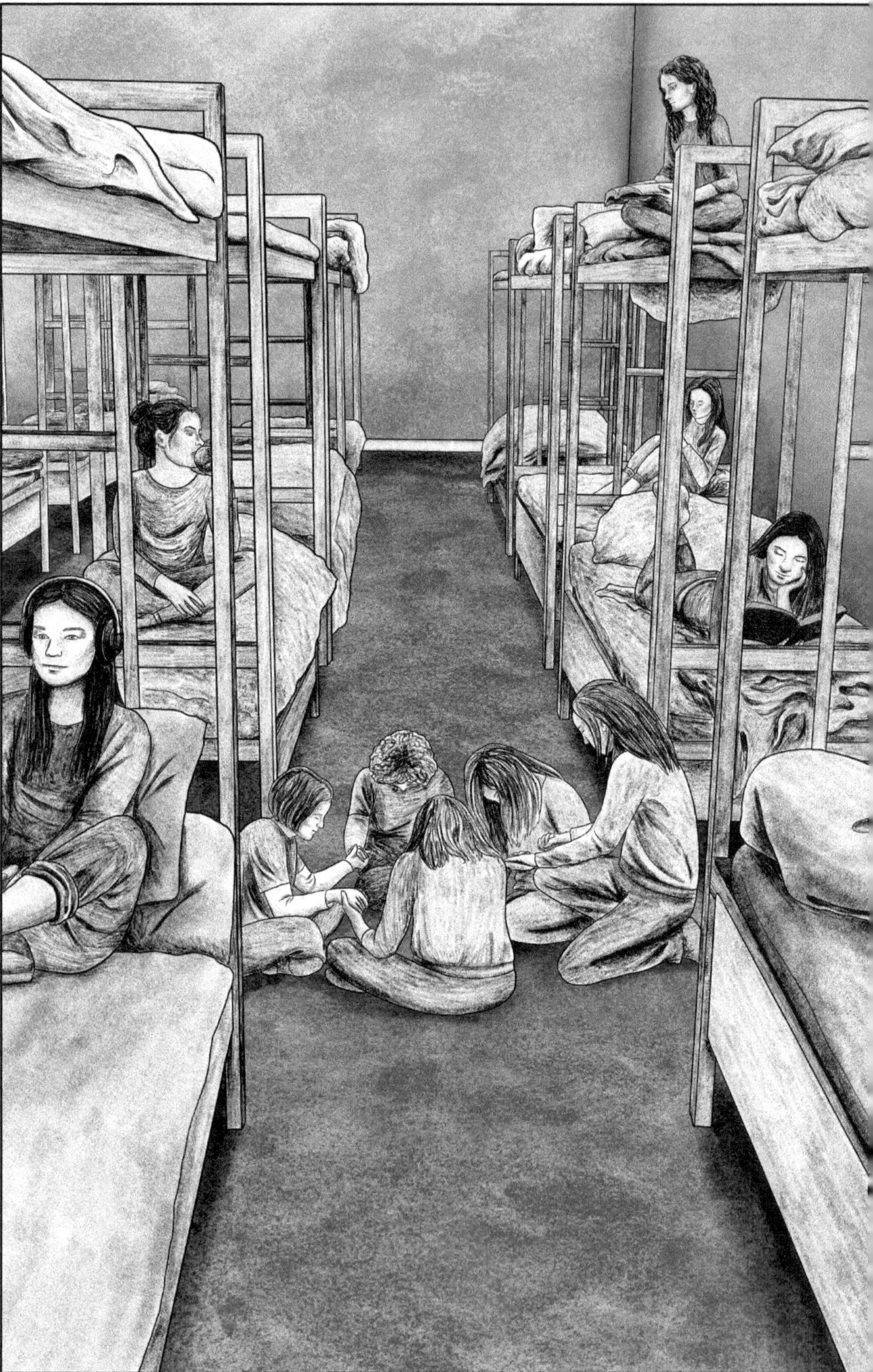

There is nothing luxurious about being in jail. I was told what to do, how to do it, when to speak, and where to go. The things outside of jail; family, relationships, finances, and a career were a hot mess and there was nothing that I could do about it to make it better. But yet, hope was rising because it seemed as if God was there with me. It seemed as if He was showing up for me. Why else would I be experiencing peace with such circumstances?

"The Lord is my shepherd; I shall not want. He makes me lie down in green pastures; He leads me beside the still waters." (Psalm 23:1-2 NKJV) There was something about this verse that impressed upon me a sense of God being in control, of Him leading me into a calmness even in the chaos of being contained and held captive to my past choices, to that part of me that I never understood, to the fear of the unknown future. But yet, the freedom that I was starting to experience I was finding in the pages of that Life Recovery Bible. Verses were being highlighted to me as if they were jumping off the page and straight into my heart. God was allowing me to lie down in this unknown green pasture, where solitude and confinement met peace and fulfillment. I was beginning to feel those peaceful streams flow within me that I had never experienced before. I was beginning to experience freedom while in prison!

I went before the judge in East Baton Rouge for my second drug charge and was sentenced to drug court. I was transported to St. Tammany parish for my first drug offense charge. I had to go before the judge that sentenced me to contempt of court when I was honest about my using, the same judge that I had skipped court on. I was scared! I met with the public defender, and he informed me that the judge was going to give me 5 years in prison. My heart sank! I expressed to the public defender that I knew I had a drug problem. I knew there was no one to blame but myself. I knew that I had gotten myself into this mess. I knew that I needed help. I asked him to see if there was any way the judge would reconsider my sentence. The judge handed down to me 5 years DOC; while suspending 4 years, but I had to do one year of prison time. I'll take it!

<h1 style="text-align:center">Question #20</h1>

What did you do when you were released this time?

There were a couple of things that I came to understand about my relationship with God. I did not trust Him, nor did I believe that He loved me. But it was evident to me that He was showing up.

I had a dream one night that I was playing basketball and the referee called me for a foul. My preferred basketball numbers in reality were either 44 or 32. In the dream, when the referee called me for a foul, he labeled my number as 45. I woke up from the dream not really understanding it because I knew that my numbers were never 45. Was it the answer to the question that I posed to God about when I would be released from jail? I did not know. I put this dream in my journal and continued living life locked up while seeking Him.

Surprisingly the guard called my name and told me to "roll up". I waited to hear if the guard really did call my name because I knew it was a little too soon for me to go home. But all inmates know what "roll up" means and when I heard my name for the second time, I knew I was going home. There was no desire to hit the streets, no desire to run back to the drugs, alcohol, money, or men. I was ready to go home and be with my family. I had already begun to allow God to start over on the inside of me, now I was ready to start over on the outside.

I was sitting on the couch with my daughter when a soft message impressed upon me to go get my journal and count the days from the day of my dream (8/25/08) about playing basketball with the number 45. I went to my journal, counted the days from the dream and it was exactly 45 days. WOW, that was the first time in my life that God answered me in a dream. I was seeing for the first time that I could trust Him.

Today is 8/25/08. Dreamed about
45 days. · Asked God to show
me when I'm getting out.
In a dream basketball. my
number was 45.
Do I have 45 days left.

I went to register with drug court and the probation/parole office the very next day after going home. I wanted to do the right things and I was putting that faith into action. The probation office gave me an appointment to return to do intake. I even started applying for jobs. Being home felt great.

I returned back to the probation office at the assigned date. When I got to the back, the officer told me to put my hands behind my back, that I was being rearrested because I was prematurely released. My heart sank! I knew I had a choice to make, a choice within myself! For the first time EVER in my life, as I was putting my hands behind my back to be re-arrested, I said to God, "God, this does not feel good, I do not understand this, but I am going to trust You!"

"God, this does not feel good, I do not understand this, but I am going to trust You!"

Question #21

Now that you were back in jail, how was this time different from the other times you were jailed?

As the corrections officer was processing my paperwork, I asked her did she have an expected release date for me. She told me that she did not but that I had 4 years of DOC time to do. WHAT!?! My heart sank! I told her that I was sentenced to 5 years but that 4 years had been suspended. I was only supposed to do one year. I imagine she has heard all kinds of things before. My mind was racing a hundred miles an hour. What will my daughter think about me being rearrested? She will probably think I did something wrong! I know my parents are going to be so disappointed! I am so disappointed myself! This is so terrible! I was doing good on the outside the few days I was home. We all were really enjoying being together. This is horrific! The only peace and comfort that I could find to slow my mind down was saying over and over, "God this does not feel good, I do not understand this, but I am going to trust You!

I was taken to the back where the dorms are located. I tried to settle in the best I could. Anxiety was in full force. Fear was daunting. Confusion was looming. But I knew one thing for sure, what the judge had sentenced me to. And he did not sentence me to 4 years. My Ma was told the judge needed to use the words concurrent instead of consecutive and my time would run together from East Baton Rouge Parish and St. Tammany Parish. Once the judge signed the paperwork, I would be going home soon.

A few weeks later, I heard the words, "Roll up Melody!" Hey.... I am going home! I was taken to the holding cell. There were other Department of Corrections inmates in this cell, and they were all excited about going to St. Gabrielle, the Women's State prison. WHAT!?! My heart sank! How can this be? I am supposed to go home! I asked the corrections officer where we were going. He did not say, but we were told to get in the van. The van started driving and as it traveled, we passed the road that led to my house! So close, but yet so far away! "God, this does not feel good, I do not understand this, but I am going to trust You!" Talking to God and declaring this over my mind and my situation was the only thing that was holding me together.

We were taken to St. Gabrielle, the women's state prison. When I sat down in front of the processing corrections officer, she began reading to me every conviction that I had ever been charged with. What could I say? Absolutely nothing because I knew I was guilty of all those charges. I did ask her what my expected release date was, and she told me that I had 4 years of DOC time to do. By this time, I was not shocked by her reply, but I was still overcome by emotions. I knew what the judge sentenced me to but that did not take away the fear, doubt and worry of what I was hearing. "God, I do not understand this, this does not feel good, but I am going to trust You!" We were placed in quarantine.

My legs were so ashy and dry they were literally hurting. I had given all my personal belongings away to some of my fellow inmates when I heard my name being called to roll up at St. Tammany because I thought I was going home. Oh, how I would love some lotion right now. I noticed a few ladies walking down the line handing out packages to inmates. I could hear other inmates referring to them as the "church ladies." The church ladies had smiles on their faces and a glow about them. They handed me a bag and I thanked them. When I looked in the bag there was some lotion! This was truly a blessing. God surely knows how to take care of us even when we have no means of providing for ourselves. I had not even asked God for some lotion, but yet, He knew I needed some. I was so grateful for the Lord. I was so grateful for the church ladies. Thank You God for being my provider!

Blessings

<h1 style="text-align:center">Question #22 and #23</h1>

Did your five-year prison sentence change your trust in God? And what did you do to combat the feelings you were having?

The great benefit about being at St. Gabrielle was having a library, being able to go to church most nights, and being able to go outside. I felt blessed to have been transported from a parish jail to a state prison even though fear, doubt and worry were tormenting factors that played on my mind and emotions. The judge had sentenced me to a total of five years DOC, but he suspended four years and I was supposed to do one year. But somehow it had gotten all twisted and I was being told that I had four years to do instead of one. God was able to use the fear, doubt and worry to move me to dig deeper into Him, into His Word. I checked out books about Christianity and spent more time talking to God because those seemed to be the only things that relieved my mind and brought some stability to my emotions.

I was given a job to work in the field. At first, I did not want to embrace it because it brought up lots of memories of being back home; expectations that I was unable to fulfill. We grew up in fields planting and harvesting many different types of vegetables. Life was great back then, but as children, we tend to take that for granted. As an adult in prison, there were so many things that I regretted when I thought of my family back home. There was a verse that caught my attention while spending time with

God, "Today is the day that the Lord has made, I will be glad and rejoice in it" (Psalm 118:24 NLT). It was as if God was saying to me, "Melody, I am making your days, be glad and sing about it!" I know that I cannot sing, but I tried. It did me good to sing that verse over my mind and my heart as I worked in the fields, and it did not matter who was listening. Walking in a structured straight line to the fields and marching back to the dorms became a place of surrender to God, just Him and me. I was not singing to please or offend the people around me, I was singing to worship God who was teaching me about forgiveness, letting go of the past, and embracing the idea that He is good all the time.

Weekends were a little different than weekdays at prison. We did not have to work in the fields on Saturday or Sunday. I started hanging out in the TV area playing cards with others. It was fun and clean. I noticed the phone ringing in the control center where the corrections officers were. A soft message was being impressed upon me every time the phone rang, "Melody, these corrections officers will need to receive a phone call for you to be able to go home. Every time the phone rings, say to yourself Melody, roll up in the name of Jesus!" I believed this was God speaking to me, informing me to take a stand of faith, declaring that I am going home soon. I was learning from the Bible that life and death are in the power of the tongue (Proverbs 18:21) and what we say really matters. I heard the phone ring again and I said, "Melody, roll up in the name of Jesus!" I noticed that I did not doubt when I spoke that. I noticed that there was a hope when I spoke that. I felt a confidence when I spoke that. Doubt, fear, and worry had no place in my mind and emotions when I spoke that. Every single time that I noticed the phone ring, I staked my faith in Jesus by making my vocal declaration, "Melody, roll up in the name of Jesus." But yet, fear, doubt and worry were there just waiting for the next crack in my armor, for fear can be vicious.

I noticed other inmates wearing straw hats while in the field. I wanted one and asked a corrections officer where I could get a hat. She replied to me that they were out of straw hats, and they were not going to get anymore. I felt cheated! How can other people get straw hats, and I cannot have a hat? To me, it did not matter that they were out of hats, what mattered is that I had just as much a right to a hat as the other women. I knew that my heart was not in the right place within myself and that having this type of attitude and perspective would not serve me well. I knew I needed God to work on my heart just like He was making my days. I asked God to help me because I did not want to be resentful and then grow bitter. "Today is the day the Lord has made; I will be glad and rejoice in it!

We made way back to the dorm from the field. It was customary for the inmates to refill the water cooler if it ran empty. Anytime this happened, one would retrieve the water pitcher, go to the supply room where the sink was located, fill the pitcher with water and take to the water cooler. Usually this would take 3 or 4 trips just to refill the whole water cooler. After my shower, I went to the water cooler to retrieve some drinking water and it ran empty on me as my cup was filling up. I remembered the customary duty of refilling the water cooler. I did not feel like refilling the water cooler!! I was tired and wanted to go lay down!! I thought about turning towards my room, leaving the empty cooler for someone else to fill and then a soft message appeared to me, "If you are faithful in the little things, you will be faithful in large ones. But if you are dishonest in little things, you won't be honest with greater responsibilities" (Luke 16:10). I knew this was a verse from the Bible that the Holy Spirit was trying to guide me with. I knew He wanted me to be faithful in this little thing. I KNEW I had a choice to make!! I retrieved the water pitcher and made way for the supply room. As I turned the corner into the supply room, something caught my attention.

It was a straw hat lying on top of a trash can!! It was as if God had placed that straw hat right there for me! I knew someone had thrown it away, but I also came to realize that God had orchestrated this moment. And it was through surrender and obedience to Him, that I was starting to experience His love for me!

Question #24, #25 and #26

In what way did you see God working in your life?

What was the event that ultimately drove you close to God?

After this event, the Holy Spirit put a vision on your heart, what was that vision?

I was starting to understand that the Holy Spirit was not to "be scared of", but that he was a person to get to know. Growing up I was raised in a very charismatic church, and I witnessed many people being "slain by the Holy Ghost", passing out, and running around church. This was scary to watch, and I did not want anything to do with a ghost as a child. Now as an adult who needed a power greater than myself not only to survive but to thrive in this world, I was open to the Holy Spirit, the power of God!

I was experiencing a one-on-one relationship with God as he continued to show up for me time and time again in that dark and hopeless place called prison. I checked out books from the library and started reading anything in the Bible that I could about the Holy Spirit. I was learning that those small voices that I had been experiencing was the Holy Spirit. I was learning that when I read verses in the Bible and they illuminate, that is the Holy Spirit bringing the Word of God alive to me personally. I was learning that when I read a passage in the Bible and it pricked my conscious and reminded me of my sinful behaviors and choices, that was the Holy Spirit moving me to repent of my sins, turn to God and ask for forgiveness. I was learning that when I experience

73

love, joy, peace, patience, kindness, goodness, faithfulness, gentleness, and self-control while in prison, that was the Holy Spirit equipping me with the characteristics of God himself.

I was learning from the Bible that it was important for others to lay hands on us in times of need and that through the Holy Spirit, God heals people. I did not like to think of others laying their hands on me, it reminded me too much of the church that I went to as a child. It was when pastors laid hands on others that they began running around church and falling out. But I knew that doubt, worry, and fear were culprits that continued to haunt me anytime I was reminded of the supposed four years that I was supposed to do. I was being tortured in my mind with doubt, worry, and fear. Even though I knew what the judge had ordered it seemed as if no one could help me, no one could correct this, figure this out, and bring this confusion to a stop.

We came in from the field and I was very tired. I wanted to wash up and lay down. I heard the corrections officer call for church. My initial thought was that I did not want to go to church. And then I heard a soft impression upon me, "Melody, go to church." I replied back, "I do not feel like going to church." And then I heard the soft impression again, "Melody, go to church." But I do not feel like going to church! "Melody, go to church." Okay, okay, I am going to church.

The sermon was on the Holy Spirit! As the pastor lady was sharing how she was having a problem with a situation in her life, she was demonstrating how she and the Holy Spirit were interacting. She asked the Holy Spirit to show her what God wanted her to know about this said problem. The pastor spoke to the Holy Spirit, "Holy Spirit, you see what is going on in this situation, show me what God wants me to see!" I was mesmerized that this pastor lady was actually demonstrating to us her encounter with the Holy Spirit. And then she began teaching about the laying on hands in times of need. She taught that when we are going through something difficult that it is good for us to ask others to lay hands on us and pray over us. The pastor lady called for anyone that needed to be prayed over to come on up to the altar. Then I heard the Holy Spirit's small voice impress upon me, "Melody, go on up to the altar." WHAT!?! "I don't think so Holy Spirit, I am not an altar girl!" And then the Holy Spirit impressed upon me again, "Melody, go on up to the altar." I had never seen these church ladies that were helping the pastor. I was scared but yet desperate for more of God. I knew I had a choice to make within myself. I got up from the pew, started walking down the aisle to a lady that I had never seen before, and when I approached her, she asked me, "What can I pray over you about?" I replied to her, "Will you pray over me for fear, doubt, and worry?" She looked at me, put her hand on my head, said a prayer, and then she spoke these words, "You are waiting on a phone call. This will all be over with soon!" WHAT!! How could she know about the phone call? How could she know that every time I heard the phone ring in the control center that I would declare within myself, "Melody, roll up in the name of Jesus"? She did not know!! For it was God speaking through her! God knew and God spoke to me, and He was letting me know, "I see you Melody, I hear you Melody, and I love you Melody!" It was in that moment when I met the love of Christ! It was in that moment, when I experienced the love that God has for me personally, for He was the only one who knew that I was waiting on a phone call.

Question #27

How was life different after being released from jail this time?

One of my sincere requests to God while being in prison was to leave prison a different person than when I walked in. He had heard my requests and was fulfilling it in ways that I could not imagine. He knew I was waiting on a phone call, and He confirmed it through that church lady.

Usually when someone is released from prison, they are released at midnight on the day of expected release date because that starts the new day. I did not have to wait until midnight to be released. I was given an immediate release because God said to release me...that His purpose had been fulfilled. I had discovered a newfound love, and I was walking out of prison a free woman, a changed woman, a woman that knew she was loved by God!

I was ready to embrace whatever God was going to walk me through, ready to go wherever God wanted to take me. I knew that I wanted to go back to that local church from that one visit that I had experienced when I was in full blown addiction. I knew I wanted to start tithing...why wouldn't I since God had been so very merciful and gracious to me? I wanted to give back to Him what was so rightfully His. I knew I wanted to go back to my parent's house where it was safe, where there was no influence of drugs or alcohol. I knew I wanted to report back to drug court and probation/parole as soon as I could. I knew I was ready to be that mommy that my daughter needed and that I needed to be for myself. And I knew I was ready to face that judge even though fear came upon me just thinking about this. But I also had learned while in prison that God is my true judge and that everything that comes my way in life must be filtered by God. I was ready and now I was given the opportunity to walk out this faith in Christ as soon as those prison doors opened. Not only was I taking me wherever I went but Jesus was coming with me also.

Question #28

Did you find a happy relationship in your life?

I knew there were things that I had to do differently if I wanted different results than the past. I was a free woman on the outside and on the inside of myself, and I wanted to keep it that way. Who I hung out with, where I took myself, who I trusted, and what truth I evaluated my life by were major elements to a healthy and satisfying godly-life. I stayed close to my family, I was focused on taking care of my daughter, complying with all the stipulations of parole/probation and drug court, and I was working hard to get back up on my feet. There were not a lot of people that I put my trust in, but the one relationship that was different, when it came to trust, was my relationship with Jesus.

I was able to save money for an apartment and two days before my birthday in 2009, my daughter and I moved into our new home. There were great things happening in the rebuilding of my life, but I still had consequences to pay for the lifestyle that I had lived. A sheriff's deputy came a knocking on my apartment door and my heart sank. WHAT NOW?!? Was I going back to prison? I knew I had done nothing wrong that was new! I opened the door and he handed me some papers. I was getting sued for breaking a lease when I was in my addiction. I also had to start paying my student loans that had defaulted. I also received a letter in the mail saying that I had to pay back money for food stamps because I was receiving food stamps when I had a drug-related felony charge. It seemed as if I could hardly breathe trying to payback all the consequences of my past.

The thought came to me to get online and find a friend with benefits. I began searching the internet but there was a gnawing in my soul and the peace that I was living seemed to be ebbing away with each search. But yet, I created an account out of financial insecurity. I knew that this choice was not the choice that God would want me to make but it seemed to be the easiest and quickest way. I toyed with the searches for a couple of weeks but could not shake the uneasiness that I felt every time I logged in to the account. I knew I had a choice to make within myself. I chose to delete the account! I would stay focused on building a relationship with Jesus and look to Him as a spiritual husband and as a provider even though fear of not having enough money was looming.

My daughter came to me and asked if her friend could live with us. How in the world could I possibly take care of another human being when I was barely staying afloat with just my daughter and me? I began praying about it and the Holy Spirit impressed upon me to put an ad in the paper advertising my housekeeping skills. I began acquiring clients. I was working two jobs: as a server in a restaurant and cleaning houses. I was attending AA meetings, had acquired an AA sponsor, was attending an out-patient program, was working a program of recovery, and attending church. Life was very busy but very good even with all the challenges. I was clean and sober, I was single, focused on Jesus and loved by God.

The hatred and resentment that I had towards my first husband was gone. God and I started working on that when I was locked up. I often wondered where Robert was, what he was doing, was he remarried, did he have other kids. Bethany would ask about him, but I could only tell her that I did not have any answers for her. With the resentment and hatred removed from my heart, I knew I still loved him!! There were so many things I wished I could have done differently when we were married but I cannot redo the past! I can only move forward while extending grace to myself over and over if need be.

I saw a mutual friend of Robert's and mine. She asked how Bethany was doing. She asked how Robert was doing. I told her that Bethany and I were doing great, but I did not know where Robert was. She replied, "He lives behind the hospital, just go down this street and it is this house." WHAT!!! My heart jumped both with excitement and fear. I was excited to see Robert after eight years of not knowing, not talking, not even seeing his face. But what was I about to run into? The one confident thought that I had was understanding that God just told me, through my friend, where Robert could be found. I was excited but scared at the same time. I got in my car, said a prayer, and headed his way.

<h1 style="text-align:center">Question #29</h1>

Now that you are clean and sober, and in a righteous position with God, what things are happening now in your life?

Physically, I could not hold up working day and night. I was hardly at home, hardly spending time with my daughter and her friend that was living with us. I was wearing down mentally and emotionally and it seemed to me that God was wanting me to take a step of faith. I knew if I quit the restaurant and focused on cleaning just houses that I had the potential to fall behind in my bills. I did not automatically have cleaning clients waiting in line and I did not have a savings account to pull from. And of course, there was no boyfriend or back pocket number to call in case I got in a financial bind. But looking back that was exactly where God could show up in the lack, in the opportunity, in the need. It was scary thinking about resigning from my server job, but I put in my notice and clung tight to Jesus while declaring His faithfulness and doing the work. And God surely was bring-ing the work to me.

I knew I needed to find an apartment that was cheaper because of having to pay back all the financial consequences from the past. I began searching and was getting denied, based on the fact that I was a convicted felon. My faith was taking a beating, but I continued to press into Jesus and continued doing the work that was right in front of me. I drove to my parent's house to visit them and noticed the house next door to theirs had been purchased out of foreclosure. There was a couple working on the house. I stopped by to see if they would be interested in renting it. The new owner said if he rented it that it would be $1,200 a month. I thanked him for his time because I knew that was more than what I was paying. I was a little disappointed, but I continued on. The next day my Ma called me and said that the gentleman who bought the house next to theirs wanted me to call him. I called him and he said, "Melody, if you are interested in purchasing the house, we will owner finance it for you. WHAT!?! I was not even looking to buy a house because I knew my credit was no good and purchasing a house was NEVER a thought. I was able to purchase the home from them, and it was cheaper than what I was paying for rent! God showed up and was definitely "showing off, as my spiritual husband and as my provider.

God-financed

Robert and I were starting to talk more. I knew there were things that he was doing that I did not want to be a part of, but yet I did still love him, and I was hoping that things would change. I was drawing boundaries for myself, and it felt good to stand up for what I wanted and needed in life. I gave him a Life Recovery Bible just like the kind that God had given me when I was locked up. It seemed as if he was wanting a different life, beginning to do some things differently, and seemed to be seeking God.

Question #30

Do you feel that God revealed to you that the only way to stay in freedom was to not take your eyes off of Jesus?

Sometimes situations are placed in front of us, and we have no clue what decision to make. We can hope to receive a Word from God from the Bible, but a specific answer to a specific question may not be there. I called my AA sponsor and told her that Robert had asked for us to live together. I told my AA sponsor that I did not know if I was making the right choice. She replied to me, "You will soon find out if you are making the right choice."

Of course, I was worried that he would relapse. I was anxious a lot throughout the day just thinking about the "what ifs". I had been reading the Bible in the mornings but now I was focused on Robert. My thoughts were about Robert, my anxieties were about Robert, and my hopes were in Robert. My focus shifted from Jesus to Robert.

I tore my rotator cuff while working out at the gym and eventually was temporarily unable to work as a housekeeper because the pain had gotten so bad. I went to the doctor; told the doctor I was in recovery and was prescribed "non-narcotic" Tramadol. I took one for the pain and surprisingly felt a little tingle from the one pain pill. It had been nearly 4 years since I had any kind of mind-altering substance in my body. I called my AA sponsor and told her that I felt a little high from one pain pill. She advised me to be careful with the Tramadol because even though they are classified as "non-narcotic", they can be addictive.

I am sure the pain was a combination of emotional and physical pain but all I knew was that I was hurting. I knew it was not time to take another pill according to the prescription. I was pondering taking another one too soon but knew that I should stick with the directions. There was a message that came to my mind, "Melody, you were able to quit smoking cigarettes and you loved smoking cigarettes. You got this! You can take another pill before it is time, you are in pain!!" This thought continued until I believed the lie! I took another pain pill before it was time. And before long, I was abusing tramadol. I knew that I was in trouble when my thoughts shifted, and I was pondering going to the doctor to get something stronger! I knew I needed to start my recovery over again. I knew I needed to make some changes in how I was processing life between Robert and me. I knew I needed to get Robert down from the throne of my heart and put Jesus back up there!! I called my AA sponsor, told her that I had relapsed, called the pharmacy, and cancelled the upcoming tramadol refill, and searched for a recovery group at my church.

Question #31

Would you recommend to others to join a church recovery group?

Growing up in a church setting, I said the sinner's prayer when I was a little girl but did not understand I was a sinner in need of a Savior. I believed in Jesus. I believed He died for me. I was that Christian who did not bear the fruit of the Holy Spirit. I was that Christian who had my agenda in mind. I was that Christian that needed to be lifted up off the ground of muck and misery and washed clean by the blood of Jesus.

God had broken the chains of enslavement off of my life in 2008. But yet in 2012, a Christian who had experienced God's love, relapsed behind a legal prescription of non-narcotic tramadol, of all things. Repentance was not far from my lips because I knew I needed my Savior. Since I was no longer a slave to the power of sin, Jesus released me from the burden of the relapse and taught me a very valuable lesson…. not to take my eyes off of HIM!!

Of course, there are moments when my eyes may wander from Jesus for I am all too human. But the Holy Spirit quickly reminds me when I am beginning to place a person, place, thing or event on the throne of my heart instead of Jesus, and I am quick to repent. Repentance may seem out of reach for some Christians, but I have learned that spiritual discernment is always predicated upon spiritual obedience to Jesus.

Question #32

After all that you've been through, when people tell you that they can recover on their own, without any help, what would you say to them?

I tried to live life on my own, doing things my way, or doing things your way, and that never worked for me. I've tried living my life focused on certain legalistic programs and placing those programs ahead of all things, but yet I always found myself in a place of struggle or complacency. It has only been when I place Christ first in my life; in my thoughts, in my past, in my day-to-day activities, in my future, is where struggle meets fulfillment and complacency meets desperation.

The very first scripture verse that I memorized while being locked up that still holds true today and shows up in a mighty big way is from Matthew 6:33, "But seek first the kingdom of God and His righteousness, and all these things shall be added to you."

It has been a mighty long time since any substance has had control over my mind, my body, or my life. I do not count my days of sobriety, for God only gives all of us each just one day. We each get the opportunity all throughout this day to choose Jesus all over again where He bestows upon us a desperate fulfillment in Him.

Question #33

Can you describe the happiness, fulfillment, and joy in your life now (with God in your life) verses your early years, and what do you do to stay pressed into God?

There has been hesitancy, anxiety, and fear behind sharing my life experiences with you. But my life is not my own and when God commanded, "We overcome the enemy by the word of our testimony and the blood of Jesus, He did not mean for us to hold on to the wrong choices and enslavements of our life but to share them with others so that the hope of Jesus can abound in them as well. For it was Jesus that brought me from death to life and it is by the power of the Holy Spirit that gives me freedom to fly.

Closing
I knew that I wanted a different life than what I was living but I had no idea how different my life would turn out to be. Sure, I still have trials, loss, temptations, frustrations, disappoint-ments, and all the emotions that go with life events, but God has and is teaching me how to surrender to Him while the Holy Spirit empowers me to be an overcomer through Christ.

God completely restored my relationships with my Daddy, my Ma, Bethany and Robert beyond anything I could have imagined. I grew amazingly close to both of my parents. I was able to par-ent my daughter like God purposed me to parent. And most of all, I was able to understand how much God loved me and that always positions me in freedom for this thing called life.

I have experienced great loss in my life; my sister died of a drug overdose, my ma died two years later and just 3.5 months later my daddy passed. Learning how to walk through life without a ma and a daddy has been hard. As the Apostle Paul had written in 2 Corinthians 4:8, "We are pressed on every side by troubles, but we are not crushed. We are perplexed, but not driven to despair. We are hunted down, but never abandoned by God. We get knocked down, but we are not destroyed."

I have also experienced great gain in my life as God has blessed me with two granddaughters who adore me, and whom I adore. There are many times when I am reminded of how, at their age, I was not there for my daughter like I am there for them. But those thoughts are only glimpses into my past because God Him-self has paved the way for restoration and redemption in ways that still amaze me not only within my relationship with my daughter, but within myself.

The cleaning business that God birthed continues to grow. It has been one of the hardest things to manage and it seems to get harder.   But I remind God A LOT that this is His business, and I will follow Him wherever He leads, even into the unknown.

The husband that I once grew to hate; I remarried, and now regard with great respect and love. Even though we are aging on the out-side, our love for each other on the inside is stronger than it has ever been. As we each grow in our relationship with Christ, our love for each other has kindled into a three-cord strand that is not easily broken. Sure, the cords sometimes get raveled, but the power of the Holy Spirit that we both have experienced in our trans-formed lives also transforms our hearts and mends our wounds.

Letting go of the past and trusting God for a future all began with one choice at a time in the present to trust Jesus. What do we have to lose if we have already lost everything including our-selves? Christ is still in the miracle making business. If you feel as though your life is too messed up and you have experienced too many losses, just hand over your broken pieces to Jesus and He will create something so beautiful that you will not even be-lieve...until you experience His great love for you!

***

Laura and I are overwhelmed by Melody's story, her strength, trials, and her willingness to share with the entire world. God has continued to bless her life. She and Robert did get back together and are in a Godly marriage today. Robert gave his life to Christ, and they have completely redeemed lives for themselves, their families, their children, and now grandchildren. Her business is thriving, and she gives hope to others wherever she goes. There is no more condemnation, no more guilt, no more influences allowed to destroy.

Melody has a vision to carry her story of salvation to whoever can benefit from it. *"For you will be rich in His love, rich in His mercy, rich in His grace and rich in His forgiveness."* If you have never taken a step of faith in Christ and asked Him to be your Savior and Lord, you can do so now… Father God, I thank you for hearing me and answering my prayer for salvation and sanctification. I ask that you save me from myself. I ask that you forgive me for not trusting you with my life. I ask to receive the Holy Spirit and be anointed with the love of Christ and the power of the Holy Spirit. I thank you that the blood of Jesus washes me clean. In Jesus' name, Amen.

Today you finished reading her story. It doesn't have to be over for you. How many times have you heard that soft voice reaching out to you, calling you? Take a chance with many others reading this right now and ask that voice to come back to you. Ask God to enter your heart and for the presence of the Holy Spirit to join you right where you are. Give all your past to him by asking him to "take it". Speak the words out loud for He waits to hear them from your lips, alone; "Lord, come into my heart", I believe in You, I believe in Jesus Christ". Speak it; "take my life into Your hands, make me a new person with a new heart starting today and lead me" In Jesus' name.

You are not alone. No matter where you are in your journey, there are other believers who can help you. Get with a local church, minister, or group. Below is a small group study that can help you understand biblically where you have been and where God is taking you. It will introduce you to the word of God and teach you about his promises. It is designed to share in a small group, but it can be completed individually.

After the Small Group section below, you will find 33 Devotions that Melody has composed and shared. The Lord has gifted Melody with her writings, as they open our eyes to the truth, and help us have a deeper understanding of Him.

***

Freedom to Fly

SMALL GROUP OR INDIVIDUAL STUDY

In Ecclesiastes 4:12, the Bible tells us that "though one may be overpowered, two can defend themselves. A cord of three strands is not quickly broken." We recommend that if conducted in small groups and you have many, that you make teams of three, if possible. Each person in a three-person team will have the roll of encouraging, the roll of expressing challenges, and the roll of praying for each other as you go through the small group study together and in the larger group. The three in your team will be your partners walking with you daily as you work on each section.

If you have accepted Jesus Christ our lord as your savior before starting this group, it will be easier for you to have faith in what you are reading, if not, we pray your faith builds to a point where you can call on God to be a part of your healing process in overcoming.

In the beginning of the book, I mention a notion and asked a question. Is your life worth fighting for? As you can see after reading Melody's story, her life now has impacted many other lives for the good. But we raised the question, is there something evil out there that is wanting to take you out before you can become prosperous, successful, and living an honorable life?

We will address this using some of Melody's story. In the recount of her childhood, she mentioned some challenges that affected her, one of which was medical and the other physical in nature. She did not like her hair and she had to deal with a unique kidney condition making her feel like she was not like other little girls. As a result, she felt less than, and unloved by her Creator. As a child, Melody believed the lie that God must not love her. The enemy was winning against her true identity in Christ.

We referenced this in the beginning of the book as buying into the big lie. To first understand how subtle this is you need to understand how Satan approaches us. He's not going to come at you from the front and kick in your front door holding a shotgun. All he's going to do is put some doubts in your head and try to get you to believe things that just aren't true. He wants you to believe these untruths and half-truths because you can then walk down a more dangerous path with him.

In the Bible Adam and Eve were commanded by God that they could eat of anything in the garden to sustain themselves. However, there was one tree from which they were not allowed to eat.
The only way to do damage in the enemy's war with God, is to harm God's chil-

dren by leading them away from Him. We can all recognize an enemy when they're dressed up like one and come at us, but not so much when it just sounds normal and possibly from a source that we trust.

Here's what happened in the Bible when Satan attempted to defile God's children, Adam and Eve.

We find it in Genesis chapter 3, verses 1 through 5.

Now the serpent was craftier than any of the wild animals the Lord God had made. He said to the woman, "did God really say, you must not eat from any tree in the garden?" The woman said to the serpent, "we may eat fruit from the trees in the garden, but God did say you must not eat from the fruit of the tree that is in the middle of the garden, and you must not touch it, or you will die". "You will certainly not die," the serpent said to the woman. "For God knows that when you eat from it your eyes will be opened, and you will be like God, knowing good and evil".

So, Satan comes from a place where he sounded like he might be just like you, not like someone trying to attack you from the front like an enemy on the battlefield, but calm and composed. In Melody's case his approach was to take her circumstances and make her question her value; to attack her in her own mind, so that she could make up her mind on other decisions based on hurt and deceit. This hurt and deceit kept her from a true relationship with God and pushed her into a singularly focused place where she needed to find something to fill the hole in her heart. Her journey put her in deathly situations, multiple times in jail, loss of a baby, marriage defiled, and facing uncertainty in her future, but God was always there! Melody's wish is that you will experience the love of Christ in such a way that when the enemy of our soul comes at you, you will be aware of the evil one's tricks by knowing the love and truth of God. You have an advantage, you can short cut the experience by calling on God and not giving in to sin that can take your life permanently.

Make a list here of the things that have made you feel worthless or just worth less. They can be things from your childhood or current day things that you are telling yourself you believe, or things you have been told to believe; anything that you remember that has stuck with you over the years.

____

____

____

____

____

____

Read Genesis Chapter 3: 1 -24

The first step of Satan is to isolate you. As in the story with Adam and Eve, Satan was sure to talk to Eve directly, taunting her that she could be just like God if she ate of the forbidden fruit. Everything he said about the fruit was true, it wasn't a lie. The fruit was good, it appeared pleasing, and it was great for gaining knowledge. Drugs and alcohol don't just appear in their worst form to you and bam you're addicted. No, they may come to you through friends who are having a good time, or escaping pain, or by observing others who seem to have life by the tail, enjoying everything that they're doing. And just like the fruit in the garden that Adam and Eve ate, it turns out there is a dark side. The path that starts out with having fun or providing a temporary escape from reality soon turns into alienating family and destroying true relationships. The addiction cycle is designed to enslave you until you are completely dead on the inside. For many, it's too late. They have lost their lives and forever impacted their loved ones.

Circle the excuses you have made to yourself, that you have bought into:

I must have a drink to be happy

I'll just do a small amount this time

I can't be myself unless I'm high

I'll never do that again

I'll do whatever it takes to get my fix

It's not my fault I did that

If (blank) hadn't happened I would not have done it

<u>List some of your own excuses below:</u>

____

____

____

____

Group Share

In your small group share some of the things you circled and listed. How do they sound to you now? Can you recognize your thoughts, and those of others in the group, as the enemy's lies that have been accepted as truths?

If you can recognize them as a lie, you have made a crucial step towards God's plan for your life. Once God enters your heart, your eyesight changes. You see things for what they are, and that small voice guiding you to do the right thing gets louder.

What do these scriptures below tell you? Review and meditate on one scripture per day this week. This is going to require effort on your part. Here's how the blessings work. You do your part and seek out the scriptures and take it into your heart, then God does what only He can do for you that you can't do by yourself. Be earnest and intentional and you will start to see His works in your life. We will be doing a good bit of this. It's a great way to receive it into your heart and your mind.

Read the scriptures below and write what the scripture is speaking to your heart. Discuss your thoughts in group share session.

Acts 2:38

Peter replied, "Repent and be baptized, every one of you, in the name of Jesus Christ for the forgiveness of your sins. And you will receive the gift of the Holy Spirit.

____

____

Matthew 6:33

"But seek first His Kingdom and His righteousness and all these things will be given to you as well."

<u>Shared by Melody:</u>

When I was locked up and began seeking God through His Word, this was the very first verse that the Holy Spirit illuminated to me. I began memorizing this verse a little each day until it became a part of me. Looking back, I can see why this verse was given to me first. As addicts, we hope to recover or save all those things that we lost in addiction, but God is wanting us to get Him first. The lie is that we must get these things first: recovery, a good job, money, a car, a place to live, getting released from jail/prison, get our children back, but God is wanting us to get to know Him intimately and then He will recover or save all that is lost according to His will for our life.

Proverbs 20:12

Ears that hear and eyes that see- the LORD has made them both

____

____

Luke 4:18

"The Spirit of the Lord is on me, because he has anointed me to proclaim good news to the poor. He has sent me to proclaim freedom for the prisoners and recovery of sight for the blind, to set the oppressed free.

---

1 Chronicles 16:11

Look to the LORD and his strength; seek his face always.

---

2 Corinthians 4:6

For God, who said, "Let light shine out of darkness," made his light shine in our hearts to give us the light of the knowledge of God's glory displayed in the face of Christ.

Acts 26:18

to open their eyes and turn them from darkness to light, and from the power of Satan to God, so that they may receive forgiveness of sins and a place among those who are sanctified by faith in me.

Receive new sight and receive God's strength. This last scripture can also be a prayer. Speak this out loud with your group.

Ephesians 3:16-19
I pray that out of his glorious riches he may strengthen you with power through his spirit in your inner being, so that Christ may dwell in your hearts through faith. And I pray that you, being rooted and established in love, may have power, together with all the Lord's holy people, to grasp how wide and long and high and deep is the love of Christ, and to know that this love that surpasses knowledge-that you may be filled to the measure of all the fullness of God.

____

____

____

These scriptures are laid out in an order to reveal to us a few things. In order for eyesight in our heart to change we must first believe that God is our savior so that we can receive the Holy Spirit into our hearts. Then we acknowledge that God created us, and he created our eyes to see and our ears to hear. By accepting Christ as our Savior our sight can be healed and we see things from a Godly perspective, as opposed to a worldly perspective. In short this is the difference between the lightness and the darkness. Hopefully you can see clearly that there is light and dark, and that the choice is yours to operate with God in the light. God wants to strengthen you and empower you to live the fullest life that you can have. Scripture references Satan as the "god of the world", for he provides all the snares that this world can offer. The Holy Spirit being inside you now, will allow you to see these snares and help you avoid them. So, this week we are praying for the eyesight of God and for the Holy Spirit to show us the things that are of this world so that we can eliminate them and shield ourselves from being part of it.

Now that you are seeing and hearing with the right eyes and ears, some things are going to change. Throughout Melody's story, we can see there were several instances of outside influences, both good and bad. The decisions that were made in between, provided the direction to either go towards God's purpose for her life or away from it. So, you may be wondering where you are in all of this right now. You know that you're about to wage a war against your past self and Satan, so you need to be equipped to make it stick.

There is a formula I used as a war veteran to determine where we are right now, and what our assets are. Now it's time for you to do the same. You have made the decision that you're sick and tired of being sick and tired of who you were, and it's time to become the person God has in store for you. You may be thinking about the people you've had in your life along the way, people who helped you, people you have hurt, and people who have hurt you. How can you put all this into perspective and turn it into an asset?

I remember a time when my son was young. He had gotten a small scratch on his hand, but to him this small scratch was huge. So, Tyler, my son, comes into the house holding his entire arm in his other hand and appears to be great pain with tears running down his cheeks as if he had a massive injury. His mother and I without much talking decided to go completely overboard on how to care for Tyler and his "massive injury". She proceeded to use every band aid and gauze in the house to wrap the tiny scratch on top of his right hand. The wrapping was the size of a softball, with five little nubs peeking out of this massive ball of gauze. At this point

Tyler was directed to go see dad. For better or for worse he was on his way from the bathroom holding his hand on top of a pillow very carefully being held up by his other hand as if it were a fresh casualty of front yard warfare.

Without missing a beat, I told Tyler that this injury was a very important injury but that he needed to go to bed as it was bedtime. Then I made a grave error in judgment and told him that if his fingers turned black, he would only have 10 minutes to live. Tyler took in this information, and we walked him to his bedroom where he sat up in his bed with his injured hand carefully placed on top of a pillow where he diligently watched his fingers to see if they would turn black. What I can tell you is that the harder you try to stay awake the faster you go to sleep, and this is exactly what happened. Tyler sat there with his head and eyes nodding forward every couple of seconds fighting to stay awake, and within 5 minutes he was sound asleep.

It was close to midnight when I checked in on him. I just happened to have carried in with me a bottle of black shoe Polish. I generously coated the five little nubs sticking out of the ball of gauze and went to bed. I was awakened around 3am to the following words: "dad we need to get to the hospital I've only got 5 minutes left to live!" We calmly walked to the bathroom sink and I began washing the shoe polish off of his hand. Then some immortal words came from my son "dad that's just not right."

I believe the statute of limitations is probably up, but there is a purpose for telling you this story. You see when we are in recovery from addiction, we believe that we have injured and hurt so many people that we are unredeemable. We think the things we have done can't be "washed" away.

Many of us may carry guilt for our actions that have caused pain to ourselves and others. But God sees it as the character-building moments of opportunity for you to ask Him to be part of your life. We may feel like the worst thing in our lives has happened but, in God's eyes, it was just a scratch. Now you must take stock of your life, and where you are, and decide to either move forward with God involved or not.

It's time to make that asset list. Take some time over the next two days and make a list of all the places and people you used to see that would lead you down a dark path. Then make a list of the positive influences in your life and the people who truly want to see you excel. These can be people in your small group that you're working with right now, they can be family and friends that have wanted to see you pull through your addiction and thrive, or some may be new or past friends who have been saved.

Step 1
Identify who the enemy is and isolate his influence on you

It may be difficult to make this list. This is a very personal thing, and some of the folks on your list that could lead you down a dark path may be considered friends. Some of the people who are on your support list who want to see you excel might consider you an enemy. This is going to make relationships complicated so we're going to uncomplicate them by looking at them through the eyes of the Bible. Realize that your true enemy is not any one person or a place. Your true enemy is the evil of the world (Satan). Let's look at some scriptures to identify who our enemy is. You know him by his actions and his influence.

(Write out the scriptures below)
1 Peter 5:8-9

____

____

____

____

Ephesians 6:12

____

____

James 4:7

____

____

John 10:10

____

____

____

Matthew 16:23

____

____

____

Compare Parallels of Scriptures written above:

____

____

____

<u>Step 2</u>

Identify who your support team is

<u>Step 3</u>

Set up an accountability partner

Read the scriptures below.

2 Corinthians 11:3

But I am afraid that just as Eve was deceived by the serpent's cunning, your minds may somehow be led astray from your sincere and pure devotion to Christ.

1 Corinthians 7:5

Do not deprive each other except perhaps by mutual consent and for a time, so that you may devote yourselves to prayer. Then come together again so that Satan will not tempt you because of your lack of self-control.

If you have made your asset and liability list this week you have done something that many will just not do. You see, if you name a thing, you can plan around it. Ever wonder why it's so hard to remember times and places that are good for you, but you know where the house is that you got drugs from that one time from years ago? Many will refuse to make an actual list that truly represents the good and bad influences in their lives. You must be serious about letting some things go and calling it what it is. Finish the week in prayer and talk with others on how they are doing with their list.

"The Rubber Band"

We will use a rubber band to illustrate the propensity towards evil or towards good; the intact rubber band representing evil. To preserve a rubber band, it needs to be kept in a dark place. The more light it is exposed to, the more the rubber band weakens and breaks down. Now we enter a time of putting your asset and liability list into play as a powerful tool. The evil of this world on one side, and God's purpose for your life on the other, and you are the rubber band! You see, you cannot serve them both at the same time. You are like a rubber band, and you are going to need to be stretched. Picture a stretched rubber band. The right side of the stretch is God's blessing upon your life and his vision for your happiness. The left side is where all that is left behind. So, the right side is what's right for you and left is where you get left behind. You can't be in both places at the same time. Just as hateful thoughts and love can't occupy the same space at the same time, both God's will for your life and the evil in this world are at opposite ends. The rubber band pulls harder the farther apart you stretch it. So, what's the secret for a win here?

Melody was radically released from the power of sin of her addiction in 2008. Melody believes that she was being transformed in processes of experiencing God's love. The lies that she had believed were being demolished, and God's truth was setting her free in moments of time, in seasons of life, and in those choices to seek Him first and above all else through the power of the Holy Spirit.

In 2012 she relapsed. Once again, she had to make a decision. It may be that you have had a relapse along the way. God still loves you and has a purpose for you. His vision and love for you is still there. The time Melody spent away was far shorter, and she knew right away this was not what God intended for her. She did get to a point of complete trust and faith in God, and maybe reading this is your chance, your second, third, or fourth…or your last. The final point where you put all your trust in Him. That's when the miracles and lessons can start to be real in your life too.

Take a moment to go read again Melody's answer to question #28. Melody had a choice. She stretched that rubber band and could have given in to the left side, and left her changed heart and mind behind but knew it would lead her to further destruction. She made the right decision and even took on more responsibility when she could not see her way, but God made a way. The result was more love, more worth, and the greatest was more armor by denying the power of the world and accepting God's direction.

Stretching the rubber band… You must stretch it wide, and the wider you stretch it, the more free you will become. The more you stretch it, the more it tries to pull you back where you can be compromised. This is where Satan wants you the most, where you are blinded from God's truths and can be influenced. Now just like any other rubber band, if you keep it stretched out, and in the light, it will soon lose its strength, become brittle, and have no power to pull you back! This is the time to rely on God's power, and not your own, to stretch the rubber band completely and BREAK IT.

Write out the following scriptures:

Psalm 59:1

____

____

Deliver me from my enemies, O my God;
Set me securely on high away from those who rise up against me.

Psalm 138:7

____

____

____

Though I walk in the midst of trouble, You will revive me;
You will stretch forth Your hand against the wrath of my enemies,
And Your right hand will save me.

Deuteronomy 20:4

____

____

for the Lord your God is the one who goes with you, to fight for you against your enemies, to save you.'

2 Samuel 22:20

____

____

"He also brought me forth into a broad place;
He rescued me, because He delighted in me.

Psalm 37:40

____

____

____

The Lord helps them and delivers them;
He delivers them from the wicked and saves them,
Because they take refuge in Him.

2 Samuel 22:4

____

____

I call upon the Lord, who is worthy to be praised,
And I am saved from my enemies.

Proverbs 16:3

____

____

Commit to the Lord whatever you do, and he will establish your plans.

Recite this prayer aloud:
Dear God,
Lord, I come to you today with an open heart, mind, and ears. Please forgive me for behaving of this world and for being lukewarm in my faith. You deserve better. I want to be better, God. I need You. Your Holy Spirit is filled with mighty strength and will. You have given me these things, so I ask that You please help me to use them Jesus. I want nothing more than to be where You are and to make You proud. I want to fully surrender my life and dedicate it all to You, Lord. Please help me die to myself so that You can give me a more refreshing and fulfilling life. Thank you for everything Lord! You bless and forgive me even when I don't deserve it.

Help me to remember that everyone and everything in the world is a small part of your Master Plan. Nothing else will truly matter. Use me. Work through me, God. I know that you are only preparing me for what's to come, which is greater than what is and what already was. Thank you, God! Amen!

"Time Fighter"

Let's talk about time. What is so special about it? Time is neither good nor evil. A common denominator that everyone on this planet has, is time. Everything that has ever been built or exists by the hands of man has been made to take up your time as value to you. Every tool ever constructed is made in some way to provide you with a benefit of time. Cars, televisions, laptops, phones, and anything else you could possibly think of is going to take, give, or use time that you have. It's no wonder every media outlet and every advertising outlet known to man capital-izes on the use of your time. Time has no monetary worth but is the most valuable commodity that you could ever have. You can't see it, but you know it is there.

What God has given us all is a "Start Time" and a "Stop Time". The in between is where we decide how our time is used. Can we use it well or fail at using it well? Of course, we can. We have two ways to use our time since God gave man "Free Will". We can use our time in a positive way, or we can use our time in a negative way. The way we use our time can affect our character, wellbeing, demeanor with others, and it is an emotional journey. We may lie to ourselves, and buy into the "Free Time" thought process. Just like freedom isn't free, free time isn't free either. We as a nation have somehow bought into a lie that there is middle ground and we created "Free (Idle) time". Let's get rid of this notion. If your choices are to spend your time doing something positive, then the rest of your time not doing something positive is what's left. Rest is rest, but idle time is an excuse to do nothing, or it can provide a way to do something negative, and both are not good for us.

In answer #32 Melody reveals her time fighting strategy. Being idle, we know, can be a dangerous place to be. So, what do we do to keep from being idle? It's time to acquire some time fighting skills. The devil will strike out at you if he sees an opening. It won't happen when you are with the people on your asset list, or while participating in wholesome functions, or while you are reading/studying your daily devotions. It'll happen when you are alone. It'll happen when you have time on your hands and aren't focused on your goals. So, what's a good recipe to become bullet proof? Stay close to your spiritual family. Have communication and conversation about your day with someone who is on your asset list, a mentor, or a sponsor.

Melody joined a small group and as of the writing of this book, she is still participating. Having continual positive influences is a plus. Being occupied with work and family in a positive way also is a plus. One thing I do know, is that Melody spends time with the Lord every day. My wife and I also start our day with scripture or a daily devotional to help us at the very beginning of the day. This is a spiritual warfare method that equips you to deal with your temptations and trials. If you set your mind right at the beginning of the day, it eases the challenges of the day and welcomes the Holy Spirit and Christ to join you during your day. Spending time with the Lord ensures that you are never alone, and that you are protected. You are protected from spending your time in ways that can harm you. When we rely on God to fight our battles, we are "Putting on the full armor of God". Look forward to this step because it will make your "Time" fulfilling, less stressful, and change your outlook to see opportunities instead of strife! You don't have to, you get to!

12
11
10
9
8

Write out the following Scriptures:

Ephesians 6:10-18

____

____

____

____

____

____

____

Ephesians 5:15-17

____

____

____

____

James 1:5

____

____

Psalm 31:15

____

____

How should we act and react? Let's review and discuss the scriptures below.

Psalm 55:16-17
But I will call on God, and the LORD will rescue me. Morning, noon, and night I cry out in my distress, and the LORD hears my voice

Matthew 6:33
But seek ye first his kingdom, and his righteousness; and all these things shall be added unto You

Proverbs 16:9
A person plans his way, but the LORD directs his steps

John 16:13
But when he, the Spirit of truth, comes, he will guide you into all truth

Psalm 12:1-21
I appeal to you therefore, brothers, by the mercies of God, to present your bodies as a living sacrifice, holy and acceptable to God, which is your spiritual worship.

Do not be conformed to this world, but be transformed by the renewal of your mind, that by testing you may discern what is the will of God, what is good and acceptable and perfect. For by the grace given to me I say to everyone among you not to think of himself more highly than he ought to think, but to think with sober judgment, each according to the measure of faith that God has assigned. For as in one body we have many members, and the members do not all have the same function, so we, though many, are one body in Christ, and individually members one of another.

What do you think Melody's strategy was?
(Write your answer based on her testimony in the answer to question 32.)

____

____

____

The writer's answer:
She stood on her faith and denied time to sin. We all have in common how easy the path is to make a bad decision. One minute of what we thought would be a good time or an escape has consequences taking a long time, sometimes years, to get over. Melody shared with us that while spending time in prison, the scripture Psalm 23 came alive to her. She said that while in prison the Lord made her slow down. God communicated with her there. Prison became her green pasture, where she became willing to listen to God, and to focus on Him. In Melody's answers to questions 22 & 23, she shows how praising God and singing even when she didn't know how, impacted her day. God kept showing up for her and he has been showing up for you too. Melody was looking at a 5-year DOC sentence. What did she do? She let God in and made Him a part of her heart. Once she let God's Holy Spirit in, the impossible was made possible. God had another plan for her. He has a plan for you too.

Read the scripture below.

Psalm 23

The LORD is my shepherd, I lack nothing.

2   He makes me lie down in green pastures, he leads me beside quiet waters,

3   he refreshes my soul.
    He guides me along the right paths
    for his name's sake.

4   Even though I walk
    through the darkest valley,
    I will fear no evil,
    for you are with me;
    your rod and your staff,
    they comfort me.

5   You prepare a table before me
    in the presence of my enemies.
    You anoint my head with oil;
    my cup overflows.

6   Surely your goodness and love will follow me
    all the days of my life,
    and I will dwell in the house of the LORD
    forever.

With the days you have this week, commit to spending some time in prayer or devotion. Podcasts are available if you don't like to read. See how doing this affects your week then share your results with the group.

Can you list at least one way that God has shown up for you? Please share with the group

____

____

____

Closing Prayer

Psalm 31:14-15
But I trust in you, Lord; I say, "You are my God." My times are in your hands; deliver me from the hands of my enemies, from those who pursue me.

"Forward Momentum and Victory"

"Lack of power, that was our dilemma. We had to find a power by which we could live, and it had to be a Power greater than ourselves. Obviously. But where and how were we to find this Power?" (AA Big Book). That statement always intrigued me, each and every time I read it.

However, I was so confused as to why I would have moments of victory in my life with a sense of value and contentment but yet mess it all up again. I believed in Jesus and had even said the sinner's prayer but being victorious over my life seemed to always be superficial, fleeting, or circumstantial. How could I grasp enduring power in my life when I was powerless?

There is a second part of that intriguing statement that goes like this, "But where and how were we to find this Power? Well, that's exactly what this book is about. Its main object is to enable you to find a Power greater than yourself which will solve your problem." The book that this statement was in reference to was the Big Book of Alcoholics Anonymous. I was able to tap into a power that enabled me to stay clean and sober for four years. But yet, here I was; back in prison (2008), back to nothing, enslaved to drugs and alcohol again, not able to care for my daughter again, not able to care for myself again, relationships broken again, and hopeless again.
I remember sitting on my bunk in jail and noticing a Big Book

of AA and a Life Recovery Bible on my cell mates bed. I knew in that moment, that I had a choice to make. I could continue on trying the same things that I have always tried, running away from Jesus, or I could seek Him and His power. I asked my cell mate if I could borrow her books. I began searching.....

"And because you belong to Him (Jesus), the power of the life-giving Spirit has freed you from the power of sin that leads to death." (Romans 8:2 NLT)

Do we believe that the power of God, the Holy Spirit, lives within us? If we do not believe that, we can stop here and ask to receive that power. "So if you sinful people know how to give good gifts to your children, how much more will your heavenly Father give the Holy Spirit to those who ask Him" (Luke 11:13 NLT). Father God, I come to You today and ask that You fill me with the power of the living God, the Holy Spirit. I thank You Father for giving me this power that now lives within me. I thank You Father that You are teaching me according to Your Word. I thank You Lord that You are working out Your purpose for my life in this very moment. In Jesus name, Amen!

We now, in faith, have the power of the Holy Spirit living within us and just like any other relationship, we must kindle that relationship. "And I will pray the Father, and He will give you another Helper, that He may abide with you forever—the Spirit of Truth, whom the world cannot receive, because it neither sees Him nor knows Him; but you know Him, for He dwells with you and will be in you." (John 14:16 NKJV).

One of the many ways that I am able to kindle that relationship with the Holy Spirit is by talking to him, just like I would talk to you. Another way is by reading God's Word. And the neat thing here is when I read God's Word, the Holy Spirit will illuminate verses within God's Word that will speak to me, encourage me, correct me, teach me, guide me and empower me. He, the Holy Spirit, will also bring to my remembrance verses from God's Word when I need them as I am walking through life. Acknowledging the Holy Spirit is just the same as acknowledging you.

GROUP SESSION REVIEW

<u>Share with each other a time or times when you know the Holy Spirit was trying to communicate with you either by pictures, impressions of words, Bible verses, life experiences or the like.</u> A lot of times we perceive these communications as our own intuition but most likely it was the Holy Spirit who was coming upon us, "You will receive power when the Holy Spirit has come on you" (Acts 1:8).

____

____

____

<u>Commit to the group that you will begin communicating with the Holy Spirit every morning asking the Holy Spirit to fill you with his power.</u> Because we have a flesh-nature (sin-nature) we will need to be filled with the power of Holy Spirit, each and every day, "Those who are dominated by the sinful nature think about sinful things, but those who are controlled by the Holy Spirit think about things that please the Spirit. So, letting your sinful nature control your mind leads to death. But letting the Spirit control your mind leads to life and peace" (Romans 8:5-6 NLT). One of the for sure ways that we can allow the Spirit to control our minds is by the renewing of our minds through the Word of God.

<u>Commit to your Lord that you will seek Him through the reading of His Word, each and every day.</u> Before you begin reading the Word of God, ask the Holy Spirit to reveal to you God's will through His Word. You will soon discover that the Holy Spirit will illuminate from those pages the verses that He will speak to you.

<u>Commit to your Lord that you will meditate (memorize) on a verse or verses (the verses the Holy Spirit illuminates to you) throughout the day.</u> We are in a spiritual battle to walk in freedom even though God has already won the war.

Conclusion

All of us fall short of God's standards, each and every day, but yet, as Christians, we have the power of the Holy Spirit living within us; teaching, correcting, guiding and empowering us according to God's will. I am a firm believer that I would not be able to live the life that God has purposed for me if it were not for the power of the Holy Spirit. I have never had confidence in myself as an overcomer, but I have been given the gift of God's confidence through the power of the Holy Spirit who helps me Overcome. "He gives power to the weak and strength to the powerless." (Isaiah 40:29 NLT)

Devotionals

When Covid hit in the beginning of 2020, I was sitting at home with time on my hands. The Holy Spirit impressed upon me to begin writing what he was sharing with me. I have never had confidence in my writing abilities, language, or grammar. As a matter of fact, I had to take speech growing up. The enemy of my soul knew my weaknesses and fears of being criticized by penning these devotionals and placing them on social media. But I knew in my spirit that God was calling me to do this. Was I going to be obedient to Him? Of course! Even in the fears, I stepped out in faith of Him and began posting devotionals on social media. The responses were touching, and I knew without a shadow of a doubt that God was building and stretching my faith in Him. My hope is that these devotionals will speak to you in a way that moves you just like He moved me through these devotionals. Before you begin reading them, please ask the Holy Spirit to reveal to you what God wants you to hear, to see, to know, and to experience according to His will so that you too, can be free to fly.

33 days of Melody's Devotionals

1. The God in the Valley

My Ma would often say, "The God on the mountain is still God in the valley." We never really understand the depth of that statement until we experience it in its entirety; until we experience the love of God in the valley.

Psalm 23 lays a visual about God being our Shepherd and guiding us through life. It is a psalm about confidence and trust. When David penned this psalm, he understood what being a shepherd meant for he tended his father's sheep.

There was a time in my life when I was made to sit still. I was caged in and could go no-where. It was one of the greatest blessings in my life because God knew my heart was ready to be taught. I remember seeing a Life Recovery Bible and asking the lady next to me if I could borrow it. I remember wanting to seek Him out of need and desperation. I remember reading the words in Psalm 23: 1-2, "The Lord is my shepherd, I shall not want. He makes me to lie down in green pastures; He leads me beside the still waters."

Did I have needs at that time? Of course, I did. Was the place that I was in a green pasture? Far from it!!! My life and that place was most definitely a 'valley of the shadow of death'.

A shadow is a shade cast by an object that is blocking light. Normally, when I hear the word 'shadow' I think of a place that is dark and scary. But according to the definition, a shadow has a light source.

"Even though I walk through the valley of the shadow of death, I will fear no evil for you are with me" (Psalm 23:4).

We may be in a valley of uncertainty, a valley of sickness, a valley of debt, a valley of fear, a valley of pride, a valley of unbelief, a valley of isolation, a valley of rejection and these valleys cast a shadow that is dark and scary. But let us take heart that these shadows have a light source who wants to guide us through these places to a place of rest and security.

Have we discovered that the shadows are nothing more than a passage to the light source of God's love? God knows the valleys that He will be walking us through. He also knows how to make us sit still while He restores our soul for the journey. "He/she who dwells in the shelter of the Most High will rest in the shadow of the Almighty" (Psalm 91:1). The shadow of the Almighty is a place of confidence and trust because we have experienced, first hand, that the God on the mountain is still the same God of the valley.

2. Scared to Write

I used to be scared to write. There were many reasons why I wouldn't even attempt it because of the messages that were being thrown at my mind. The Bible calls these messages the 'fiery arrows of the enemy.'

I have learned that these arrows were strategies from the enemy in an attempt for me not to write, much less post for all to see (and potentially be criticized). The messages went something like this, "Melody, you never made good grades in English", "Melody, you had to take speech when you were younger", "Melody, what do you know about writing", "Melody, who do you think you are!"

When Covid began in 2020, I had more time at the house, and began penning and posting a few writings. Just to think of posting in public brought about a sense of anxiety and fear, but I knew that God was calling me to do it. The one recurring message that the Holy Spirit continued to pour over me was to just take that step! To step out in faith and trust God!

Is God calling you to a place that seems like the dark abyss of the unknown? Is the enemy throwing fiery darts at us in hopes that fear will prevent us from stepping out? "Hold up the shield of faith to stop the flaming arrows of the evil one" (Ephesians 6:16).

The Holy Spirit communicates with me in pictures and words. When the enemy throws those darts of lies at me, I see myself holding up the Word of God as a shield. This shield protects over my life, my mind, and extinguishes all the flaming arrows of the enemy. The fiery darts do not stick, they fall away. God's purpose prevails in that moment and courage rises up and steps out.

Let us take inventory and ask ourselves a few questions....
Has God been calling you to step out in faith?
Have we practiced obedience to that calling?
What miracles have you witnessed because of your obedience?
What lives have you touched?
Has God proven to be faithful to you?

Does fear rear its ugly head when I know that I am about to step out in faith? Of course, fear comes! Is faith there? It better be! For faith in God is the only way to overcome the enemy's schemes. For the thief comes only to steal, kill and destroy God's purposes for our life (John 10:10). But Jesus comes and His purpose is to give us a rich and satisfying life.

"Arise, shine; for your light has come, and the glory of the Lord rises upon you!" (Isaiah 60:1).

3. Life Jacket

The other day I posted a picture of my sister diving mightily through the air from the top of our swimming pool ladder. Her courageousness was visibly perfected in the moment. I, on the other hand, had a life jacket on in waist deep water. My sister made a comment that I used to dive from the bottom rung of the ladder with my life jacket on. I believed what she said but I could not remember that moment.

A few days later, I went into the attic to try and locate a picture of daddy with his mule. To my pleasant surprise, I came across the picture of me doing exactly what my little sister said...diving with a life jacket on, in waist deep water, from the last rung of the ladder... oh my word! I could hardly believe my eyes.

How could I have gone from an obvious scared little girl to a woman that is willing to follow the Lord wherever He leads me? Does that mean I am void of fear? Absolutely NOT!

Being scared is human. I have experienced many moments of fear no matter how valiant it may look on the outside. We all get in situations where fear begins speaking louder than our faith. What I do with fear becomes the trajectory of my life.

God called Gideon to deliver Israel from the Midianites. God also told Gideon to reduce his army from 32,000 men to just 300! The Lord said to Gideon, "You have too many men for Me to deliver Midian into their hands" (Judges 7:2).

I am sure Gideon felt quite inadequate for the battle, maybe even outright fearful. But God had a plan like He always does, "In order that Israel my not boast against me (God) that her own strength has saved her, announce now to the people, 'Anyone who trembles with fear may turn back and leave Mount Gilead'" (Judges 7:3).

"When the Lord sees that men would overlook Him, and through unbelief, would shrink from perilous services, or that through pride they would vaunt themselves against Him, He will set them aside, and do His work by other means." (Matthew Henry Commentary).

As I was reading through Scripture this morning, the Holy Spirit gave me a gift…. today, I wear that same life jacket. And even though I may feel scared inside, I am still willing to take a leap of faith and dive into the pool of life believing that my God will save me, deliver me, and uphold me to conquer the land that He is guiding me through. My life jacket for life is Jesus. And even though there is plenty of fear within me, faith in Jesus becomes the saving grace for my life.

4. I do not know what to do!

A vast army is coming against you! What is your initial response? To whom do you turn to first?

King Jehoshaphat was informed of a great multitude coming against him, and his people, and he was alarmed. Feared, Jehoshaphat set himself to seek the Lord (2 Chronicles 2:3 NKJV).

Just like King Jehoshaphat, you and I are leaders of people, leaders of our family, our communities, citizens of our great nation. What do we do when fear of death, financial disaster, slander of our country, illnesses, division of loved ones, deception and hate comes a calling?

I felt like I was in a tornado getting thrown about in every which of a way and not knowing what to do. The Holy Spirit reminded me of the verse in 2 Chronicles 20:12, "I do not know what to do, but my eyes are on You (Jesus)." Relief of tension came over me, but for a moment. As soon as I realized the problems were still there, I tensed back up.

Was there more in the scriptures in relation to this verse that the Holy Spirit is trying to get me to? I opened up my Bible and began reading in 2 Chronicles 20.

A leader should know what to do. A leader should have a plan. But King Jehoshaphat stood among the crowd and openly vocalized to his people that he did not know what to do. Is he incompetent? If someone was leading me and they told me that they did not know what to do while a vast army was coming against us, I would be terrified. But isn't this how most of us feel, even as leaders, when crisis hits!

To me, this is where miracles happen; when we come to the end of ourselves, even as leaders, and admit that we do not know what to do, but our eyes are on You Lord!

5. Chosen to Seek Him

Even if we believe that God is the appointer of mankind, this does not automatically relieve us from the accountability of God's choosing. "Then King David turned to the entire assembly and said, 'My son Solomon, whom God has clearly chosen as the next king of Israel, is still young and inexperienced. The work ahead of him is enormous, for the Temple he will build is not for mere mortals—it is for the Lord God himself!'" (I Chronicles 29:1 NLT)

In 1 Chronicles 28, King David had every detail planned for his son Solomon to carry out in the building of the temple. To me, this is a picture of how God has already planned every detail for our life, for our nation, for our families, and He is wanting to pass that wisdom on to us. "I will establish his kingdom forever if he is unswerving in carrying out my commands and laws, as is, being done at this time" (I Chronicles 28:7 NIV).

King David had hoped to build the temple himself but that was not God's plan. For God had chosen Solomon, King David's son, to build His temple. Sometimes we have no clue what God is up to in our lives, in our families, in our nation. But we have come to believe that He is faithful to fulfill what He has chosen for our good and His glory for us who follow Him (Romans 8:28). As a matter of fact, King David posed this question for the great task at hand, "Now, who is willing to consecrate himself today to the Lord?"

The word consecrate in the concordance of my study Bible means to set apart or devote to God. It is not our responsibility to try and fulfill other people's calling that God has chosen for them. But it is our responsibility to carry out that calling that He has chosen for us. For He may have chosen us to give our time, our talents, our resources, our expectations, our hopes, our mind, our heart, our life…those things that He has given us.

The journey ahead may seem daunting, questionable, and unfavorable to our way of life. But God is not asking us to figure out His plan, He is asking us to carry out His will. "And Melody, my daughter, learn to know the God of your ancestors intimately. Worship and serve Him with your whole heart and a willing mind. For the Lord sees every heart and knows every plan and thought. If we seek Him, we will find Him. The Lord has chosen us to build a Temple as His sanctuary. Be strong, and do the work" (1 Chronicles 29:9-10). For God is building that temple that begins within us.

6. Holy Spirit Inventory

Taking a personal inventory of myself was never at the top of my to-do list in the past. But I have learned it is a vital part of being able to live a life of freedom. We made a searching (fact finding) fearless (fact facing) moral inventory of ourselves (Part of Step Four in the Big Book of AA).

One of my reasons, early on in recovery, why I did not like taking an inventory was because I would need to rehash some hurtful things in life. Truth, in itself, can be hurtful. Especially when we see something in ourselves that we do not like and has not benefited us in any way.

In the concordance of my study Bible, to search, means to investigate or examine thoroughly. How am I able to properly investigate or examine my own heart?

"Search me, O God, and know my heart; try me, and know my anxieties; and see if there is any wicked way in me" (Psalm 139:23 NKJV).

When I am walking through life and something begins to bother me, I will stop and ask the Holy Spirit to search my heart to see if there is anything within me that stands in the way of God's will for my life. I also ask that if he finds anything to reveal it to me. He is very consistent in fulfilling that request!!

In Psalm 139: 19-22 (NIV), David was communicating with the Lord. "If only you, God, would slay the wicked! Away from me, you who are bloodthirsty! They speak of You with evil intent; Your adversaries misuse Your name. Do I not hate those who hate you Lord, and abhor those who are in rebellion against You? I have nothing but hatred for them; I count them my enemies." Sounds like David is in a predicament, but yet he stops and asks God to search his heart (Psalm 139:23 Search me, God, and know my heart; test me and know my anxious thoughts.)

There will be moments in our day when we will face certain thoughts, certain emotions, certain temptations, certain events, certain habits, certain sins. "Let US search out and examine our ways and turn back to the Lord" (Lamentations 3:40 NKJV). The greatest blessing in all of the inventories that I have taken is to have been taught that I need the Holy Spirit to search and examine my heart, for I fail miserably at doing so myself. And one of the greatest gifts that I have been given is being able to walk in freedom. To God be the glory!

7. *Master Builder*

Today, October 5, 2020, makes 6 years that Robert and I have been remarried. These six years have been a time of rebuilding, restoring, redeeming and relearning how to have a successful marriage according to the ways of the Lord.

We met in 1993 and for the first couple of years, it was all fun and partying. Hardly a care in the world and living life to the fullest according to our definition of what that looked like. We were more concerned about building the kind of life that we wanted that we failed to see what was really important, building a life with Christ as our foundation. "Is it a time for you yourself to be living in your paneled houses, while this house (of the Lord) remains a ruin?" (Haggai 1:3).

There was much bitterness, hurt, fear, and living for self that ended in divorce years later. "We expected much, but see, it turned out to be little. What we brought home, God blew away. "Why?" declares the Lord Almighty. "Because of My house, which remains a ruin, while each of you is busy with your own house" (Haggai 1:9).

It was not until ten years later that God would place us back in each other's lives. What had changed?

Now this is what the Lord Almighty says, "Give careful thought to your ways (Haggai 1:5). You have planted much, but harvested little. You eat, but never have enough. You drink, but never have your fill. You put on clothes, but are not warm. You earn wages, only to put them in a purse with holes in it (Haggai 1:5-6).

The work that we put into building the first marriage did not grow in value. We finally came to the end of ourselves. We needed a house that could withstand the elements of life, the many facets of our diverse hearts, and the rewiring of our thoughts. We knew we needed a master builder. "They came and began to work on the house of the Lord Almighty, their God" (Haggai 1:14).

These last six years this new house has been filled with hurt, sadness, fear, anger, and grief. But it is being rebuilt with surrender, courage, humility, forgiveness, grace, mercy and the hope of Christ. The master builder, Jesus, holds the blue prints while Robert and I continue to allow Him full access to our hearts so that He can build a home that is worthy of any storm.

8. Light in Darkness

When I look back over my life there have been many times I was blind and could not see. I could not see my sin, I could not see how I hurt others, nor could I see how much Jesus loved me. These are just a few of the areas that I was blinded to, there were many more.

"Satan, who is the god of this world, has blinded the minds of those who don't believe. They are unable to see the glorious light of the Good News" (2 Corinthians 4:4 NLT).

Yesterday I was talking with a lady and we were sharing some of our life experiences. I shared with her how in 2008 I had absolutely nothing. I did not have a working car, a roof over my head, relationships were typically superficial, emotional and spiritual security were circumstantial and Jesus had no place in my life. I remember even believing that I could call God a she if I wanted to....It was my right to call God what I wanted. I hardly called upon God at all, until of course, I needed his help while in a fox hole.

My Ma used to tell me, "Melody, the only way that Satan can get you is to deceive you." I was so full of myself; my own desires, my own ways, my own beliefs, that I was blind to the truth of Christ. But because of His mercy, His grace and His unconditional love for me, He continued to pursue me even though I could not see Him.

"For God, who said, 'Let light shine out of darkness, made His light shine in our hearts to give us the light of the knowledge of the glory of God in the face of Christ" (2 Corinthians 4:6 NLT).

I do not have a magical formula to define how the light of Christ made way into my life. But I do know one thing for sure...I was down to nothing because everything else that I tried, made for a miserable God. That, in itself, was a blessing.

Even though my life today looks so much different than 2008, God is still shining His light into areas of darkness. I need Christ today just as much as I needed Him when I was void of that life-giving light. I need Christ to shine His truth into the world's deceptions that try to invade the light of Christ in my life. "We are pressed on every side by troubles, but we are not crushed. We are perplexed, but not driven to despair. We are hunted down, but never abandoned by God. We get knocked down, but we are not destroyed" (2 Corinthians 4:8-9 NLT). Through God's mercy we have this ministry, we do not lose heart!! When we feel as though we are at the end of a rope, it is Christ, who is our light and hope.

9. The Row to Hoe

Growing up, daddy had a mule named Annabelle. Many a summer we planted and harvested acres of gardens. Many a people enjoyed the fresh vegetables from the garden. But only a few understood the work that went into the delicious bounty.

Jesus knew that he would face persecution and death in Jerusalem, but he was determined to go where God had called him. "As the time approached for him (Jesus) to be taken up to heaven, Jesus resolutely set out for Jerusalem" (Luke 9:51).

Most times, when God asks us to do something, the row to hoe is hard, unbroken, and bumpy. We tend to want the journey mapped out, boundaries established, roads smooth, and harvest ripe and ready for the taking. As a matter of fact, we would be happy to have others pick the bounty for us.

Sometimes we have friends and family with us in the field of life that are guiding us to take the short cut because the work is too much to bear and quite uncomfortable. Jesus replied, "Foxes have holes and birds of the air have nests, but the Son of Man has no place to lay his head" (Luke 9:58). God has not called us to live a life of comfort but to follow Him at all costs even when the field is barren and untouched.

Sometimes there are huge boulders in the field that must be dug up before the row can be hoed. Most often these boulders have names written on them like rejection, bitterness, envy, greed, unbelief, and fear. Digging these stones out of the ground makes way for planting the seeds of Gods righteousness.

We can't plow looking back over where we have been, for we will plow a crooked row. But what does looking back mean and why is keeping our focus on Jesus important? There are things in my past life that at some time or another, seemed like a great idea or tickled my fancy, but was not fit for a king, a King named Jesus. Plowing requires a single-minded focus and so does following Jesus.

The cost of full surrender to Christ for you may be different than it is for me. Nevertheless, the plumb-line remains: "Anyone who starts to plow and then keeps looking back is of no use for the Kingdom of God" (Luke 9:62). I am one blessed woman to partake at the table of my Lord's obedience where the row to hoe was hard for Him (Jesus) but conquerable because His eyes were on the Father.

10. Oh my Soul
Why are you cast down, O my soul, and why are you disquieted within me? (Psalm 42:5)

I have been taught that my "soul" means my mind, will and emotions, my thoughts, my choices and my feelings.

This will be the first Mother's Day, May 2020, without my Ma; So heartbreaking!! I can sense my soul drawing colder in my thoughts and my feelings. And to top it off, I want to draw away from my Heavenly Father.

It is easy to think upon all the things that have gone wrong. It is easy to allow my feelings to override the promises of God especially when the circumstances of life seem daunting and relentless. But then the Holy Spirit reminds me that I have a choice; a free will.

Oh, my Soul, what will you choose?

Will I focus on all the confusion of this world? For God said in I Corinthians 14:33 that He is not the author of confusion but of Peace.

Will I focus on the fact that Ma will not be with me to celebrate Mother's Day? For God said in 2 Corinthians 5:8 that to be absent in the body is to be present with the Lord. Ma is celebrating with Jesus!

Will I focus on the fact that there are promises that God has given me that He has not kept? For God said in Isaiah 60:22 that when the time is right, I, the Lord, will make it happen.

Will I focus on the fact that I do not feel like doing life today? For God said in Nehemiah 8:10 that the Joy of the Lord is my strength. Ah yes....the enemy of my soul is not trying to steal my joy, he is trying to steal my strength; my God-given strength. The enemy of my soul is seeking to make me ineffective for God's Kingdom.

As I type and look up bible verses and declare them over myself, I can sense the fight of faith welling up in my soul. I am reminded of the question in Joshua 24:14, "Choose this day, whom you will serve!" Will I serve self or my God?

Thank you, Jesus, that when I turn away from You, You chase me down with Your goodness and Your grace. Thank you, Jesus, for always being so very good to me.

11. He is Faithful

I am a member of a small group for business leaders through my local church. This week's lesson was on Faith at Work. I consider myself a woman of strong faith in Christ mainly because I have experienced His transforming power in my life.

Do you consider yourself a faith-filled person? Does your faith in God wane from time to time? You are not alone!

My daughter posted a picture of my second grand baby acknowledging Scout's 6-month milestone (April 2020). As I pondered the information my thoughts were with my parents. My Ma died the day before Scout was born. Wow....my Ma has been gone 6 months. My daddy followed right behind her just 3 months later. Soon after my Daddy died, I thought to myself that maybe life will get back to somewhat "normal". What a delusion!

How can life be normal under all these circumstances from grieving two parents, trying to sell a house, trying to buy a house all the while trying to navigate life during this pandemic of uncertainty and fear. Needless to say, I've been feeling quite faithless lately.

I turned my thoughts to the lesson about Faith and began to dive in. There wasn't much about the faith lesson that I had not heard or experienced but there was one question that confirmed how faithless I felt. "What situations in your life or business do you need to have faith for God to come through?" I began crying, "I NEED FAITH FOR GOD TO COME THROUGH FOR ALL AREAS OF MY LIFE!!!"

Does my faithlessness make God unfaithful? According to His word, it does not! Romans 3:3 says, "What if some did not have faith? Will their lack of faith nullify God's faithfulness? Not at all!" My faithlessness just means I need Jesus! For He is the champion who initiates and perfects my faith (Hebrews 12:2). Does this make me a candidate for a miracle in all areas of my life? I believe so!

12. Standing on His promise

Yesterday I received some news that was very devastating, "Mortgage companies are pulling all bank statement loan programs during this time of a fluid market". So, the loan that we were in the process of acquiring for my parent's home is no longer available.

As soon as I read the email, I literally felt nauseous because this approach was our last option. I knew I needed to be with the Lord, so I began talking to Him, telling Him how I felt; scared, angry and sad. But then He reminded me, "Melody, we've been here before! What promise did I give you about your parents' home?"

Several months ago, we started the process of trying to acquire a mortgage loan. My husband and I are both self-employed. We were getting denied based on a traditional tax return program due to debt/income ratio (student loans can come back to bite you!).

So, we tried a different approach through a bank statement program. We were approved but the interest rate was so high we could not afford the mortgage payment. At that time, my hope of buying my parent's home was slipping away. I went to my desk, sat down, and asked the Lord for a word, I said, "Lord, you have not given me a word about my parents' house to stand on. I am asking that You give me something to stand on." I pulled out my devotionals and my Bible and began seeking Him. At that time, my husband and I had just moved into my parent's house so we could work on getting our house sell-ready to put on the market. We had been living; (sleeping/lying) in my parent's home for about 2 nights.

As I am reading devotionals, the devotionals are referencing Bible verses. So, I went to the Bible and began reading the chapters of the referenced verses. It had referenced me to Genesis 28. As I am reading about Jacob's dream, I came across this verse and it jumped off the page and slapped me in the face... Behold, the Lord stood above it and said, "I am the Lord God of your father, Isaac, and your grandfather, Abraham. The ground that you are lying on I will give to you and your descendants!!" There it was!!! A promise from God for me to stand on. I knew it was for me because my husband and I were now "lying" in my parents' home.

I took that promise and I began mediating on it, writing it down on my bathroom mirror, writing it on my heart, renewing my mind when doubt came. It also gave me a new resolve to keep seeking. I was later directed to another lender that would ulti-mately approve us through the bank statement program with a lower interest rate; one that was doable to us.

Fast forward, now here we stand during this Coronavirus that is affecting EVERYONE, including the only option that we had for a mortgage loan. BUT WE HAVE BEEN HERE BEFORE! Do I be-lieve God is faithful to His word? Am I going to stand on the promise that He already gave me?

I have no clue how God is going to work this out. I am doing my part; processing with my husband, my spiritual mentor, my sib-lings, a few others, praying but most of all I am standing on, clinging to, and believing in the promise that Jesus gave me concerning my parents' home, "Behold, the Lord stands above it (the Coronavirus, the banks, the loan, the houses, and myself) and said, 'I am the Lord God of your father and grandfather. The ground that you lie on, I am giving to you and your descendants.'"

13. God's Economy

Every single one of us is being affected by the coronavirus. Our lives seem to have been turned upside down and it was not because of something we did to cause it. IT CAME....

So here we stand, facing fear, facing the unknown. Facing words like death, limited this, or limited that, and recession. When one is in the process of selling a home, recession is not a likable word.

I know there are some that are fighting for their physical lives, fighting for emotional well-being, fighting for some kind of financial security and fighting the fight of faith. All of us are fighting for something.

At the moment, my family is no longer sick. However, we are fighting the fight of grief, finances, disappointments, challenges as small business owners, and fighting for the heart's desire to sell one house in order to buy my parent's home. Being able to buy my parent's home means so very much to me.

I sat down at my computer and began working on QuickBooks, and the word "recession" was like a dripping of constant annoying water. I could not get the words out of my mind. Then, all of a sudden, the Holy Spirit brought to my remembrance a time in my life during the last recession.

It was the beginning of 2009; I was living with my parents trying to start over in life. I saved money for an apartment and was in the process of moving out on my own. I was a single mother determined to stay focused on Jesus. He was teaching me how to look to Him as my provider; my everything.

One day, I was about to go look at an apartment for rent when my Daddy said, "Melody, why don't you keep staying with us! We are in a recession, and it will be hard to make it out there on your own. You can continue to save money and it will be safe here with your ma and me." I remember looking at my Daddy and saying, "Daddy, I am learning to walk in faith and not fear."

I had no clue that I was going to make it on my own when I spoke those words to my Daddy. But I did learn one thing! … That Jesus had been so very good to me, and He never changes.

While I pen this experience, I am once again reminded of God's faithfulness to me. How the Holy Spirit brought to my remembrance God's faithfulness in spite of a recession, in spite of illnesses, in spite of grief, in spite of financial insecurity, and in spite of myself.

14. Promise Keeper

This morning while strolling Ripley and Scout, it was announced on K-Love radio that one of the most equally stressful events, likened to a divorce is selling and/or buying a house. Once I acknowledged the emotional sentiment of that struggle, I smiled because God's timing is impeccable.

At the ending of 2019 my husband and I began the journey of submitting our applications for a home loan in order to purchase my parent's house. We were denied several times through the process. However, we were approved for a bank statement program with an interest rate of 6.5%. We proceeded on because it was our only option in purchasing my parent's house. Then, the pandemic of fear hit, and everybody's life changed!

In April, I posted on FB how the mortgage loan was pulled because the investors were no longer funding the bank statement programs due to all the uncertainty of the pandemic. I penned how disheartened, discouraged, and depleted I felt.

There were many of you who encouraged me by commenting with love and faith. There was one comment that went like this, "I am on the edge of my seat waiting to hear how God has worked this out and how it turned out better than expected." When I read that comment, I thought to myself, "This option was our only option. I do not see how this will work out better."

I was so heartbroken from grieving losses to being rejected, faith was hardly on the horizon. Looking back at those moments of loss with despair, disappointments, and depletion, I am certain of two things; God not only held me together with His grace, but He strengthened me to take the next step towards Him....and the next and the next step.

There were moments that all I had to hang onto was the promise that He had given me about this house, "I am the Lord your God, the God of your grandfather and the God of your father. The ground that you are lying on I will give to you and your descendants" (Genesis 28:13).

We kept trying, in spite of all the fear that was before us, around us, and behind us. Today, the Lord has fulfilled His promise to me. My husband and I are official owners of my parents' house. And to top it off, God went above and beyond by providing an interest rate for a conventional loan of 3.875%. Jesus is the Promise Keeper!

15. Your Life a Bible

My Ma used to tell me, "Melody, your life may be the only Bible someone reads." There have been many years of that life that I would not want anyone to read much less be an example for. But God surely knows how to take a broken, delusional life and create something beautiful.

God surely needed to change my heart, so that my life, be worthy of reading.

"You show that you are a letter from Christ... written not with ink but with the Spirit of the living God, not on tablets of stone but on tablets of human hearts." 2 Corinthians 3

What do people read when they look at our lives? What words define our moments? What statements highlight our seasons? What theme does our Book of Life portray?

"I will give them an undivided heart and put a new spirit in them; I will remove from them their heart of stone and give them a heart of flesh (a responsive heart to God)." Ezekiel 11:19.

There are many moments in my life when I have the opportunity to stay resentful, become bitter, stay angry, live in self-pity, and be defiant of where God is walking me through. Emotions are a part of life but are not worthy sentiments to live by. But it is in these moments, where I lay my heart upon the sacrificial alter of the Lord and say, "Here I am Lord, have Your way with me!"

I have learned through enough disobedience and outright defiance that to kick against the goad of God's will for my life brings about a solidifying of the heart where His love seems distant or nonexistent.

"But as for those whose hearts are devoted to their vile images and detestable idols, I will bring down on their own heads what they have done, declares the Sovereign Lord" (Ezekiel 11:21).

I often tell people, the denial of my addiction never kept anyone from seeing the truth about my life, but it kept me from accepting that truth. None of us are able to keep God's standards perfectly. We all need a Savior whether we are in denial of this or not.

Our life speaks volumes not only to others but to ourselves if only we will surrender to Jesus and ask the Holy Spirit to search our hearts. For if Jesus laid his life on the sacrificial alter of the Lord, do we think we are exempt from doing that also? Denial and delusion have no place in the Kingdom of the Lord but in a heart made of stone.
No longer will God's people seek many idols, we will be content with the One true God. For it is He who has written our names in His Book of Life.

16. *The Master Teacher*

Ripley loves yogurt covered raisins in the individual boxes. We were watching a movie when I noticed, upon completion of eating her raisins, she opened her hand and released the empty box onto the floor. My first thought was, "Oh that is cute, she thinks she can throw her trash on the ground." I asked her to pick it up. She ignored me. I pushed the issue, she pushed back. My next thought was, "She does not know better. She has yet to be taught that she cannot throw her trash in my space. I must teach her." I decided to model it for her. I picked up the trash and threw it in the trash can.

The next day, I observed her doing the same thing; upon completion of eating her raisins, she opened her hand and released the empty box onto the floor. I said to Ripley, "Oh no, we are not going to trash up our space." I asked her to pick it up. She ignored me. It dawned on me that she is learning to exert her will. She is learning that she can decide for herself, and she is telling me with her actions that she is NOT going to pick up her trash. Thus, the journey begins…I must teach her.

Life is like that with us and God. He wants to teach us something new; something for our good; something that does not trash up other people's space without their consent. But we will have none of it. We have learned to exert our will. Thus, the journey begins…God must teach us.

"When I refused to confess my sin, my body wasted away, and I groaned all day long. Day and night Your hand of discipline was heavy on me. My strength evaporated like water in the summer heat." (Psalm 32:3-4 NLT)
I took ahold of her little hand, placed her hand on the empty box and walked her over to the trash can. She kicked and screamed through the whole process. As soon as I released the box from our hand, I began clapping for Ripley, cheering her for a job well done. She did not think it was funny or exciting.

Sometimes, God wants to teach His ways to us, but we kick and scream through the whole process. But then there comes a time when we realize that this is for our good and His glory. We come to understand that He is trying to clear away those trashed up areas in our life and within ourselves.

"Oh, what joy for those whose disobedience is forgiven, whose sin is put out of sight! Yes, what joy for those whose record the Lord has cleared of guilt, whose lives are lived in complete honesty!" (Psalm 32:1-2 NLT)

Are there areas in our life where we know God needs to take over and teach us His ways? One day, Ripley will celebrate with me. At the end of the pain-staking process of surrendering our will, we will appreciate that God took ahold of our hand and guided us the whole way. The Lord says, "I will guide you along the best pathway for your life. I will advise you and watch over you." (Psalm 32:8)

17. Leap of Faith

She called out to Him (to Jesus) but He did not answer. She was desperate because her daughter was struggling and suffering by a demon spirit. She believed if she could just get His attention, something good would happen. But Jesus did not say a word to her. The only reply she heard was His disciples urging Him saying, "Send her away! She is following us and making all this noise".
(See Matthew 15:22-23)

Jesus finally answered, "I was sent only to the lost sheep of Israel" (Matthew 15:24). Did He speak up because he was irritated at the disciples' remarks? Did He speak up because no one else would help her? Did he finally answer to see if she would take another step of faith towards Him even though they were so different from each other?

As I pushed Ripley in her swing, I could tell she was contemplating something. She stretched out her leg, pointed her toe downward and began dragging her foot on the ground to slow the swing just a bit. I said nothing. I knew what she was about to do because I too, had done the same thing before when I was a little girl. I watched, hoping she would take that leap of faith and jump out of the swing. I knew, if she fell, I would be there for her.

The Canaanite woman was persistent in seeking after Jesus, even though she was so different than He, even kneeling down before Him, "Lord, help me!"

We may think we are not good enough or wise enough to receive the blessings that God has for us just because we are different than other people. Jesus even challenged what this Canaanite woman really believed by saying, "It is not right to take the children's food (blessings) and toss it to the dogs" (Matthew 15:26 GNT). But the woman of faith was desperate. "That's true sir," she answered, "but even the dogs eat the leftovers that fall from their master's table" (Matthew 15:27 GNT).

Even if this woman was afraid, she stepped out and took that leap of faith. She pointed her foot and stretched her leg towards Him because she was a woman on a mission. She finally heard the words that her hurting, aching heart was searching for, "You are a woman of great faith! And at that moment her daughter was healed." (Matthew 15:28 GNT). Are we dragging our feet trying to slow down the pace of life? Are we afraid of jumping into the unknown to go where we have never gone before? Even in the silence; He is watching, He is waiting for us to step out and leap towards Him.

18. Babes in Christ

Scout is barely over a year and already walking. Her walk is clumsy and crooked, kind of how we as baby Christians look, as we fumble with temptation even though our salvation has been paid for.

We had a sin debt that we could not pay but was deemed not guilty in the court of righteousness because of Jesus. For this, we are called Children of God. "I write to you, dear children, because your sins have been forgiven on account of His name" (I John 2:12).

As little children in the Kingdom of God, we all begin our journey stumbling over sin. But faith in God begins to stabilize us as we keep taking one step at a time, one day at time, growing in our understanding of who Christ is and who we are in Christ.

Even though Scout can barely walk, her specialty is climbing and attempting things that makes no sense. She climbs fearlessly. She slides from great heights even though the landing does not look pretty. She does not allow the stumbling in her gait to deter her attempts to greater things.

"I write to you, young men/women, because you are strong, and the word of God lives in you, and you have overcome the evil one" (1 John 2:14). Who doesn't want to believe that we are growing in our relationship with Christ? We like the notion that we are wiser, stronger, and more stable. The Word of God says that when we keep His commandments (1 John 2:3) and not hate our brothers and sisters, not only do we know the Lord, but there is nothing in us that will cause us to live a lifestyle of stumbling (1 John 2:11).

Each stage in our spiritual life builds upon each other. "And the Lord who is Spirit—makes us more and more like Him as we are changed into His glorious image" (2 Corinthians 3:18).

There will come a day when Scout's walk will be graceful and filled with strength and stability. For she will have grown intimately in her relationship with Christ where she understands that no matter what life brings, Christ has been with her from the beginning… "I write to you earthly fathers and mothers, because you have known Him who is from the beginning and it has been He, that has set us free…free to live indeed".

19. Put on the Armor of God

As soon as Ripley walked through the door, I noticed something was different about her. Maybe it was the bright colors, or the horn that was protruding forth but regardless, it caught my attention.

"Put on"....were the two words that the Holy Spirit gave me as soon as I saw Ripley's hat. I was also given the verse that immediately follows ....."Put on the whole armor of God so that you will be able to stand firm against all strategies of the devil" (see Ephesians 6:10-20).

Apostle Paul, who penned Ephesians 6, was likely chained to a Roman solider while in prison for sharing the Good News of Christ. The Holy Spirit gave him this visual description of putting on the different pieces of God's armor from the armor of the Roman solider. While God gives us the power of the Holy Spirit who lives within us, He also gives us His armor that surrounds us for the spiritual battleground.

"Guard your heart above all else, for it determines the course of your life" (Proverbs 4:23 NLT). According to the MacArthur Study Bible, the "heart" commonly refers to the mind as the center of thinking and reason (See Proverbs 3:3; 6:21; 7:3), but also includes the emotions, the will, and thus, the whole inner being. To guard, we must put on the armor of God. Ripley at some point while getting dressed for the day, put on her unicorn hat.

It was such a beautiful morning, I suggested to the girls that we take a walk. Ripley hopped on her tricycle and Scout hopped in her red car and off we went. Ripley began riding so fast that the tricycle got away from her and off the tricycle she flew, falling to the ground. Of course, there were some moans and groans as she got up from the pavement, but her unicorn hat was still intact on her head.

There have been times in the past when Ripley would get tired and not even want to ride the tricycle anymore; leaving me to carry it. As soon as Ripley got up from the pavement, she grabbed her tricycle and began pulling it towards home. Did Ripley's fall change the fact that she was capable of riding a tricycle....NO! Did Ripley's fall give an opportunity for her to get back up and instead of giving up, persevere on with her armor in place (hat)....YES!

As soon as I noticed what was happening I began cheering for Ripley and letting her know that I was so very proud of her. God is cheering for us today and He is proud of us for putting on His armor in preparation for the battle ahead.

20. Growing in Adversity

"Is it even worth it", my husband asked me? He was referring to owning and operating a small business with all the challenges that business owners experience, especially now.

Ezekiel knew exactly what day, what place and whom he was with when he felt the hand of the Lord take hold of him, "In the thirtieth year, in the fourth month on the fifth day, while I (Ezekiel) was among the exiles by the Kebar River, the heavens opened, and I saw visions of God" (Ezekiel 1:1 NIV).

Soon after my husband and I finished our conversation, I went to my desk, began looking at some figures and entertained the question that he asked me, "Are all the challenges and time that I put into the business, worth it?"

I have been so overwhelmingly busy this year that I have not stopped to look at the numbers. I was amazed at how God continues to grow His business. But it does NOT feel like I am growing! Sometimes, it feels quite the opposite; like I am failing. And that is when the Holy Spirit impressed upon me God's truth, "Melody, the numbers are not what is growing you, it is the adversity that God is using to grow you!"

"Then the Spirit came into me (Ezekiel) and set me on my feet. He spoke to me and said, "Go to your house and shut yourself in. There, son of man, you will be tied with ropes so you cannot go out among the people. And I (God) will make your tongue stick to the roof of your mouth so that you will be speechless and unable to rebuke them, for they are rebels. But when I give you a message, I will loosen your tongue and let you speak." (Ezekiel 3:24-27 NLT)

WOW...this is too much!!! God is talking about being tied up and zipping the lip!!

I have often said in our recovery group, "I need God just as much today with years of recovery as I did on the days that I was en-slaved to substances." Has our prosperity, prestige, status quo, or intelligence blinded us to our need for God? Ezekiel knew that God had called him to this vision, and he was willing to turn his will over to the care of God no matter what he had to experience or go through.

There are many moments of time that people do not see when I am working. There are many moments of time that people do not see when I have gone into my house and shut myself in to just be with the Lord. There are many moments of time where I zip my lip and allow God to speak to me through His Word. There are many moments of time when I am hesitant to turn my will over to the care of God because it feels as if I am being all tied up in ropes. There are many moments of time that I do not understand how God is growing me until I encounter ad-versity, and I see that He is with me and that He is so worth it!

21. God's Goodness

Ripley spent the night with us on Friday night. I was excited to bake cinnamon rolls for Ripley on Saturday morning. I mean, what kid does not love cinnamon rolls!?!

The cinnamon rolls not only looked yummy but smelled yummy.

I was even excited to eat some as it had been a long time since I enjoyed a cinnamon roll (or three).

I chopped a cinnamon roll up, placing it in a plate in front of Ripley. She just stared at it, poking at it…turning her nose up to it. As soon as I saw her reaction this thought came to my mind, "If Ripley would just taste the cinnamon roll, she would know that it was good!" Immediately the Holy Spirit impressed upon me Psalm 34:8, "Taste and see that the Lord is good."

As God's children, we may believe that we will go through life with less trials and afflictions but that is far from the truth. In Psalm 34, David uses words like; troubles, brokenhearted, fears, and crushed in spirit to describe his situation. David is hurting, he is running for his life, but yet his greatest need is to taste and see that the Lord is good in the midst of the madness.

We may find ourselves staring at monthly expenses that far exceed our income, we may hear of test results with a prognosis that grips the heart and the spirit, we may have a prodigal child where hope grows dimmer with each passing event, we may experience pain on a daily basis, or be holding onto a dream that we worked so hard for that is slipping away. But yet, in Psalm 34:9, David proclaims to himself, "Those who fear the Lord lack nothing, the lions may grow weak and hungry, but those who seek the Lord lack no good thing!"

Have we tasted the Lord's goodness? Do we long for more of Him? No matter what we are facing today, we do not have to face it alone. For when we cry out, we know that He hears. No matter what we have gone through, we have experienced His deliverance. No matter the brokenness, we have felt His closeness. And even when we our spirits are crushed, He saved us. (Psalm 34:17–18)

Will we pick up our fork and dive into His goodness, into His faithfulness, into His love...will we take refuge in Him? Yes, we will...for we have tasted and seen that the Lord is so very good to us even in the madness of life.

22. The Contender of our Lives

One of the greatest blessings that I have chosen to grab ahold of is being able to care for my granddaughters while their mom goes to work. Caring for two babies, 14 months and 33 months, can be a real challenge but most rewarding as well.

For the most part, my house is child proof but there are a few things that are Me-Me's and not Ripley and Scout's. Still, they do try their best to get away with treating these items as their own when I am not around. It reminds me of how I used to be before I met the love of Christ. I wanted what I wanted and did what I wanted to do without regard of what God thought or said. Do I still want what I want...of course!! But do I do what-ever it is that I want to do...of course not!

The Lord says, "I will guide you along the best pathway for your life. I will advise you and watch over you. Do not be like a sense-less horse or mule that needs a bit and bridle to keep it under control" (Psalms 32:8-9).

Some of us have had to learn the hard way...through consequence and discipline, especially when we are kicking against the goads of God's purpose for our life. "Many are the woes of the wicked, but the Lord's unfailing love surrounds the one who trusts in Him" (Psalms 32:10).

Once Ripley and Scout learn that they cannot do what they want with a specific item, they inevitably move on to the next item on their agenda. We all contend with a flesh nature, but thanks be to a loving God that He is always contending with us, for He knows the plans that He has for our lives and wants to teach us according to that plan.

Ripley and Scout are learning that they cannot have their way in everything that they want at Me-Me's. But they also know that even when they break something while exerting their wills, I love them just the same. "For You, Lord are my hiding place; you protect me from trouble and surround me with songs of deliverance" (Psalms 32:7).

23. The Storms of Life

Yesterday as Ripley, Scout and I were playing on the back porch a storm came barreling through. There were two different reactions from the girls when the thunder roared about. Ripley continued to play but yet Scout came running towards me, eager for me to pick her up and hold her in my arms.

"My thoughts are nothing like your thoughts, says the Lord. And my ways are far beyond anything you could imagine" (Isaiah 55:8 NLT)

It seems to be good when one feels confident as it can be quite appealing to the human eye. Ripley's courage to not run when the thunder rumbled seemed inviting and contagious. Ripley even went towards the rain that was falling off the house to play in it. "The rain and snow come down from the heavens and stay on the ground to water the earth. They cause the grain to grow, producing seed for the farmer and bread for the hungry" (Isiah 55:10 NLT).

There were so many years of my life that I thought I knew what was best for me. It only took a little storm, here or there, to come barreling through my life to prove otherwise. But yet, it was in the running to my Father, that He was able to pour His truth (His Word) into me, producing in me, His thoughts and His ways.

"It is the same with My Word. I send it out and it always produces fruit (love, joy, peace, patience, kindness, goodness, faithfulness, gentleness, and self-control). It (God's Word) will accomplish all I want it to, and it will prosper everywhere I send it" (Isaiah 55:11 NLT).

Before the storms were over, Scout began playing in the rain with Ripley. Watching them hold out their arms and allow the rain to wash over them was a sweet reminder of how God's Word will wash over us if we will just run to our Father. For he will pour over us His truth, strength, and power in a way, that we will be able to stand in and walk through any storm of life.

24. Syncing with the Holy Spirit

Jesus said in His Word for us to be of good cheer, that He has overcome the world (John 16:33). Believing that Christ has already overcome this world can seem a bit outlandish with all the heartaches that surround us. For some of us, we may think we are experiencing new trials in life. But in God's reality, there isn't anything that this world has experienced that He has not already defeated.

"They will put you out of the synagogues and make you outcasts. And a time is coming when whoever kills you will think he is offering service to God" (John 16:2 NIV). Right after Jesus warned his disciples that they would experience persecution and death, Jesus also stated that He would be leaving them. I would question my leader if he told me these things and then left me! But Jesus also told them that it would be for their good that He was going away, for if He did not go away, the Counselor would not come.

"I (Jesus) tell you the truth, you will weep and mourn while the world rejoices. You will grieve, but your grief will turn to joy" (John 16:20). There are many trials in life when loss seems to be our only companion. I am sure when Christ was crucified, the disciples thought that all was lost. I imagine the enemy was whispering in their ear, that what they believed was a lie. Peace and comfort must have eluded them while hopelessness made way to their heart.

In John 14:18, Jesus promised the disciples that when he left, he would not leave them as orphans; all alone, not having anyone to teach them.

"But when he, the Spirit of truth comes, he will guide us into all truth" (John 16:13). Who is teaching us? Do we allow the Holy Spirit to take us by the hand and guide us into the territory of Christ? A territory of hope, of peace, of comfort, of unexplainable joy even in moments of excruciating pain! "For the world cannot accept him (the Holy Spirit) for it neither sees him nor knows him, but we know him, for he lives in us and will be in us" (John 14:17).

We don't have to conquer this world to be overcomers of it. For Christ already overcame it and we have the Holy Spirit living in us, who guides us through it. We do not have to be in sync with this world for we are in sync with Christ.

25. Holy Spirit Fruit

Do circumstances rob us of the fruit of the Spirit; love, joy, peace, long-suffering, kindness, goodness, faithfulness, gentleness and self-control? (See Galatians 5:22 NKJV). We may be going through hard times, heart break, grief and sadness, but the fruit of the Spirit does not fall off our tree. "You will know them by their fruit. Do people pick grapes from thorn-bushes or figs from thistles?" (Matthew 7:16 NKJV)

One of the things that my Ma told me is to not put my eyes (trust) in any human being (including myself) before the Lord. She understood the importance of not looking to humans as a god, because she had been hurt by doing so. "Cursed are those who put their trust in mere humans, who rely on human strength and turn their hearts away from the Lord. They are like stunted shrubs in the desert, with no hope for the future" (Jeremiah 17:5-6 NLT). Stunted shrubs have no growth and are unable to produce fruit, especially in circumstances that are not favorable to the shrub.

"But blessed are those who trust in the Lord and have made the Lord their hope and confidence. They are like trees planted along a riverbank, with roots that reach deep into the water. Such trees are not bothered by the heat or worried by long months of drought. Their leaves stay green, and they never stop producing fruit" (Jeremiah 17:7-8 NLT).

We may go through times in our lives where we feel dry, living in a barren land, parched from the elements, and wonder when our fruit will develop. But fret not, it is the Holy Spirit's job to develop this fruit in our lives.

When we keep our eyes on the prize; trusting Jesus more than humans, the fruit of the Spirit will begin to mature... fruit that tastes good, is nourishing to our soul, and appealing to others. For the Master Gardener knows exactly what type of fruit we need for the exact season that we are in, and His helper, the Holy Spirit, will develop this fruit in us because we trust our lives to Christ!

26. Picking up the Word

The other day I was outside with Ripley and Scout playing by the swing set. Ripley was holding some blocks while trying to climb the steps to the slide. She dropped a block on the ground and immediately began crying. One would think that she would step down the ladder and go get her block...but she froze, overwhelmed by emotions, just looking at her lost little block.

I thought about picking it up for her because she was still on the steps. But I knew this was something that she could and should do for herself, even if she had to climb back down. So, I said to her as she was crying, "Ripley, go pick up your block!"

She climbed down the stairs...still crying...walked over to her block...still crying...picked up her block and immediately stopped crying. At that exact moment, the Holy Spirit impressed upon me that this is how I used to be...overwhelmed by emotions in life until I learned that all I had to do was pick up God's Word and He would calm me with His truth.

No matter what, we can rely on the truth of God's Word to navigate us through life. Looking back, I can see one of the reasons why I did not want to read the Bible. "For the Word of God is alive and powerful, it is sharper than the sharpest two-edged sword, cutting between soul and spirit...exposing our innermost thoughts and desires" (Hebrews 4:12).

I knew that my convictions did not line up with His truth and reading His Word would bring to light those dark places. But it was those dark places that God's Word brought to life when I became desperate enough to seek Him through His Word. Now we can stand confidently knowing that His Word, by the Holy Spirit, is what guides us through life no matter what we face!

27. Enjoy the Ride
Many months ago, I purchased a tricycle for the grand babies. I knew they were too young to know how to ride but I purchased it anyway. With Ripley being the older of the two, I knew she would be the first to learn how to ride it, if she wanted to.

Ripley was curious about this red thing that Me-Me brought home. She touched it, rang its bell because that was very easy for her to do, and tried to get up on the tricycle. Her little legs were too short and not strong enough to hold her steady and I am sure she withdrew out of fear.

"Let us draw near to God with a sincere heart and with full assurance that faith brings, having our hearts sprinkled to cleanse us from a guilty conscience." (Hebrews 10:22 NIV).

It was easy to not approach God because of my guilty conscience. I knew the life I was living was not how I was supposed to be living therefore faith in God was fleeting. But He was there; waiting on me, hoping that I would approach Him; give Him a chance, try Him out.

Because I knew that Ripley was unable to get on the tricycle by herself; I would pick her up, set her on the tricycle, place her hands on the handlebars, and push her around. Once her legs were long enough to touch the peddles; I placed her feet on the peddles, pushing her feet down on the peddles, saying aloud, "Push your feet Ripley", while moving the tricycle in a forward motion. I did this because I love her, I want to teach her, and I want her to enjoy all the good things of being a kid.

"Let us hold unswervingly to the hope we profess, for He who promised is faithful" (Hebrews 10:23). Once I experienced God's faithful love over my life, it changed the trajectory of my heart. I had experienced what His love and hope felt like, and I wanted more.

Once Ripley grew a little more, she was able to get on the tricycle by herself. She was able to push the peddles just a little but not going too far and would easily give up in frustration. "And let us consider how we may spur one another on toward love and good deeds" (Hebrews 10:24). I am sure I have looked like a crazy woman with all the cheering that I give my grand babies as I try to encourage them forward. Sometimes God encourages us to move forward, and it may seem as if He is asking us to do more than we are able to do. But there He is...cheering us on in love, hope, and faith.

"So, do not throw away your confidence; it will be richly rewarded. You need to persevere so that when you have done the will of God, you will receive what He has promised" (Hebrews 10:36).

The first day that Ripley was able to ride the tricycle in a distance, by herself, was on Feb 2nd. Yesterday, she got on the tricycle and began riding so well that the back wheel of the tricycle was coming off the ground. It was a beautiful moment seeing her laugh and zip around on her tricycle with joy, unlike how she was unable to do before.

28. The Kindness of God

Ripley is 19 months older than Scout. They remind me so much of Becky and me, as we are 17 months apart in age. Ripley and Scout do everything together and have a visible bond of love towards each other.

A while back when Scout was playing with a toy that Ripley wanted, Ripley would snatch that toy away from Scout, leaving Scout to cry. To me, this was unacceptable behavior. I drew a line in the sand and every time Ripley snatched something from Scout, I would take it back from Ripley, telling her that her sister was playing with this, and I would return the toy back to Scout.

The other day, I was watching them play and I noticed something different that Ripley was doing. Instead of snatching the toy out of Scout's hand, Ripley placed a toy into the free hand of Scout, while removing the desired toy from Scouts other hand. Scout fell for it hook line and sinker!

The word manipulate is not in the Bible, but the book is filled with stories of people who are manipulators. Manipulators tend to try and control or coerce another person for one's own advantage. As a matter of fact, I too was a huge manipulator, until of course, God started transforming my heart. All of us humans can be tempted to do whatever it takes to get our own way. "For everyone has sinned; we all fall short of God's glorious standard" (Romans 3:23 NLT).

I am sure there will be many life lessons that Ripley, Scout and I will be involved in, and I take this role very seriously and consider myself blessed to be a part of their lives! Even though, I have to correct manipulative behaviors between the two, I also pour into their life goodness and kindness because I love them so much. It reminds me of God's goodness and kindness when He was teaching me about my manipulative behavior and transforming my heart. "Don't you see how wonderfully kind, tolerant, and patient God is with us? Does this mean nothing to us? Can't we see that His kindness is intended to turn us from our sin?" (Romans 2:4 NLT). For it is by His mercy that He withholds His judgement and by His grace that He transforms us from our manipulative ways.

29. Hidden Treasures

When I take the grand babies with me on a trip, we typically pick up something to eat along the way. This serves a couple of purposes; their attention is on the food, and they are less likely to become fussy about being in the car seat. I always hold the food! As they finish with what they have, I hand out to them more food to eat.

"This, then, is how you ought to regard us: as servants of Christ and as those entrusted with the mysteries God has revealed" (I Corinthians 4:1 NIV).

Yesterday as I put each girl in her car seat, I dug in the bag and handed to them a potato wedge. And then I made a big boo-boo! I gave the whole bag of potato wedges to Ripley! I got in the car and drove away. As Scout and I finished our potato wedge, I asked Ripley if she would give her sister and me a potato wedge? Ripley shook her head, said NO and pulled the bag of potato wedges close to herself.

As Ripley was demonstrating to me her authority, the Holy Spirit impressed upon me a picture of the relationship between God and me. God holds the bag of His secret things and when we are ready to receive what He has to offer, He will hand out to us those things. But if He prematurely hands us a bag of His goodies before we are spiritually mature enough to steward them, we will have the tendency to declare those things ours and pull them close to ourselves. "Now it is required that those who have been given a trust (entrusted with the things of God) must prove faithful" (1 Corinthians 4:2 NIV).

There are many secret things that God has given me. He has given me His salvation, His power, His comfort, His faithfulness, His peace, His wisdom, His strength, His forgiveness, His redemption, and His love. Do I hold onto these things and not share with others? Will He be able to hand out more of what He has so that He can work through me?

"What do we have that God has not given us? And if everything we have is from God, why boast as though it were not a gift?" (1 Corinthians 4:7 NLT). Is my life comprised of talking a good talk or does my life demonstrate His power through me? "For the Kingdom of God is not a matter of talk but of power!" (1 Corinthians 4:20 NIV). Do I hold these secret things that God hands to me close to myself or am I willing to share with others?

30. *Wanderers or Sojourners*

The other day I noticed a t-shirt that someone had on, "Not all who wander are lost." It reminded me of the time when I used to wear a t-shirt with that saying on it. I had another t-shirt that I wore with a proudness, and it went like this, "Well be-haved women seldom make history." I loved those t-shirts!

During the times that I wore those shirts I was walking life out by my own beat of the drum. Yet, still today, it takes courage to stand up for what we believe in and sometimes that means look-ing as if we are lost. It takes a strong-willed woman to fight a good fight of faith...whatever that faith is in.

"I heard an unknown voice say, 'Now I will take the load from your shoulders; I will free your hands from their heavy tasks. You cried to me in trouble, and I (Jesus) saved you" (Psalm 81:5b-7a NLT).

This morning while reading in Psalm 81, I came across a verse and it jumped off the page, "So I let them follow their own stub-born desires, living according to their own ideas" (Psalm 81:12 NLT). God is such a good God that He will not hinder our deci-sions and will allow us to stand up for what we believe in and fight a good fight of faith...whatever that faith is in. Oftentimes, it was those decisions that created the heavy loads, heavy tasks, and trouble that I did not see coming until I found myself en-tangled by my own walk of life.

"Oh that my people would listen to Me! Oh, that Israel would follow Me, walking in My paths! How quickly I would then subdue their enemies! How soon my hands would be upon their foes" (Psalm 81:13-14 NLT).

We will have enemies and foes no matter which path we take, no matter what decisions we make, no matter what we stand up for, or no matter what faith we believe in. But Jesus delivers a promise for those of us who are found in Christ that He will subdue our enemies and that His hands would be upon our foes establishing them as He sees fit. And He will become a familiar voice to us as He establishes our walk of life.

31. <u>Watering the weight with the Word of God</u>

Ripley grabbed the watering pail and set off for the water hose. She wanted to water the flowers. I was adding water to the pail when I realized I may have added too much for her strength. As soon as I turned the water hose off, she picked up the watering pail and made way for the rose bush. In her strug-gle to carry the water pail she shouted out, "It is heavy!"

"At that time Jesus answered and said, 'I thank You, Father, Lord of heaven and earth, that You have hidden these things from the wise and prudent and have revealed them to babes.'" (Matthew 11:25 NKJV)

Even Ripley, in her child-like mind, understood and cried out when that thing she was carrying was too heavy; when that thing did not make sense to her; when that journey was too much for her to make on her own without the help of a power greater than herself.

"Then Jesus said, 'Come to Me, all of you who are weary and carry heavy burdens, and I will give you rest.'" (Matthew 11:28 NLT) We have often been told that the Lord will not give us more than we can bear. But I beg to differ. I believe God allows us to take on more than we can bear especially if we are trying to do things in our own strength, in our own way, in our own arrogant wisdom, for He wants nothing more than for us to turn to Him for His spiritual strength and wisdom.

"Take my yoke (His Word) upon you and learn from Me (Christ), for I am gentle and lowly in heart, and you will find rest for your souls. For My yoke is easy and My burden is light" (Matthew 11:29-30 NKJV).

Christ is such a gentleman that He will step aside and allow us to man-handle things on our own if we choose to do so. As Ripley was pouring the water out onto the roses, the Holy Spirit impressed upon me this, "See Melody, as the Word of God is poured out upon the circumstances of life, the load gets lighter to bear."

32. Godly Wisdom

I started experiencing excruciating pain to the point of being nauseous. My husband took me to the ED (now called Emergency Department) and I was diagnosed with a kidney stone as the primary source of my pain and a minimal concern in another area.

As someone who is in recovery and values my recovery, I am very cautious as to what I put in my body, no matter if it is a legal prescription. However, I was hurting so bad, I knew I needed relief. I also knew that with a kidney stone, pain usually lingers around the corner until it passes. I was sent home with a few prescriptions, one that included a pain medicine.

When my Ma was alive anytime I had a surgery that required pain medicines, I always had a back-up plan that included her holding my medicine.

One may wonder, "Why would someone that has years of quality recovery need someone else to hold their medicine?" I have learned that pain and pride coupled together can manifest into a double-edged sword that can shred me to pieces. "Pride goes before destruction" (Proverbs 16:18).

My plan included asking a family member to hold my medicine.

I am not trying to win over grandiose thinking that I can handle this situation on my own. I know I need people in my circle that are supportive in my recovery and not for my dysfunction! I know that I need Jesus!

We may believe that we're above it all, a god unto ourselves, accountable to no one including God! King Nebuchadnezzar thought that he was the most powerful ruler on earth until he found himself eating grass, driven from all that he knew, and humiliated because of his pride (Daniel 4). But the pain of his situation stirred up within him, a desperation for God. "After some time (in his dysfunction), King Nebuchadnezzar looked up to heaven, his sanity returned, and he praised and worshiped the Most-High and honored the one who lives forever'' (Daniel 5:34).

It amazes me how Jesus continues to work for the good in my life; in pain, in pride, in fear, and in desperation. He is there guiding us along the way, if we will let Him. Honoring Jesus with my life is, to me, the highest priority that I take very seriously. In return He takes great care of my recovery.

33. She Will Come to Know!
If she only knew….

Ripley loves to play in the rain. It is amusing to watch her hold out her little bitty arms while standing still in the rain and allowing the water to wash over her. It's as if she has no cares in the world.

If she only knew….

Once the rain is gone, her attention turns to the water puddles. She splashes about, seeking out the next puddle. It's as if life is full of fun.

If she only knew…

Ripley has a newfound toy…the umbrella. It does not even have to be raining for Ripley to run around the yard with the umbrella over her head. She does not understand that the purpose of the umbrella is to protect her from the rain. For she does not think about needing protection.

If she only knew….
If she only knew that life would be hard, would she want to grow up.

But oh, what a beautiful day that will be when she finally understands the truth of God's love for her!

For she will come to know His strength.

For she will come to know His peace.

For she will come to know His protection.

For she will come to know His comfort.

For she will come to know His guidance.

For she will come to know His saving grace.

And though the storms of life will come, she will come to know that He will be everything that she needs.

Reference Page

Alcoholics Anonymous (4th ed., pp. 45). (2001). We Agnostics. New York:
   Alcoholics Anonymous World Services, Inc

Matthew Henry's Concise Commentary, Judges 7:1-8

MacArthur Study Bible (1997). Tennessee: Thomas Nelson, Inc.